'...the hidden languange of cities, in which buildings are nouns,
the inhabitants verbs, and empty spaces adjectives in an
endlessly changing narrative'

ZACHARY MASON, THE LOST BOOKS OF THE ODYSSEY, 2011

A HOUSE IN THE CITY

home truths in urban architecture

Robert Dalziel and Sheila Qureshi Cortale

Edited by Tim Battle

RIBA Publishing

A HOUSE IN THE CITY

© Robert Dalziel and Tim Battle, 2012

Published by RIBA Publishing, 15 Bonhill Street, London EC2P 2EA

ISBN 978 1 85946 452 6

Stock code 77536

British Library Cataloguing in Publications Data
A catalogue record for this book is available from the British Library.

Commissioning Editor: Lucy Harbor
Designed by Ashley Western
Printed and bound by W & G Baird Ltd

RIBA Publishing is part of RIBA Enterprises Ltd.
www.ribaenterprises.com

CONTENTS

FOREWORD

The UK's housing crisis is acute and it is growing. Here in London more than 30,000 new homes a year are needed just to keep pace with a population that will soon outstrip its 1939 historic peak. What kind of housing will be fit for purpose, and where should we look for inspiration?

Most cities are defined less by their great architectural monuments, public buildings or civic parks, and rather more by the homes and neighbourhoods that form the bulk of their urban building. Depending on their quality, residential streets, squares and estates define and delineate the boundaries of both our private and public lives, profoundly influencing each to flourish or fail. This new and fascinating study of housing designs and layouts from nine cities in five continents is a highly topical source book that illuminates the ways we can achieve housing that inspires, endures and minimises its environmental footprint.

The London case studies in Chapter 11 conclude, perhaps inevitably, that the Georgian town house and the 19th-century mews home score highest as efficient, adaptable and attractive typologies. In contrast, much postwar housing – despite being the product of highly specified and conscious design – has struggled to adapt to the stresses of urban change. At current rates of house-building, new homes need to last longer than Stonehenge, yet almost all the housing being replaced today is less than 50 years old. Can looking, learning and adapting the legacy of earlier successes and failures help us do better?

A House in the City is produced by authors who are putting their evidence and learning into practice as builders of the 'rational house'. This book, and their new homes, are welcome and tangible examples of why our current housing crisis needs inspired solutions.

DAVID LUNTS
Executive Director, Housing and Land
Greater London authority

INTRODUCTION

The idea that it might be possible to summarise the many complex, subtle and technically demanding issues relevant to today's housing may seem over ambitious. But we believe that it is important to try, as the providers of modern housing have put themselves in a position where an understanding of the many influences on the design of individual homes, and also of the urban spaces between them, cannot be superficial. Before the 20th century, the fabric of cities often arose organically and informally, and was subjected to continuous review and reappraisal. But now, the regeneration process is largely in the hands of professionals and development agencies (public and private) whose time frame is necessarily abbreviated. A point made by N J Habraken regarding architectural intervention is very relevant: "practices historically developed to create unique and limited acts of monumentality cannot guide us in engaging the commonplace".[1]

Should the aspirations of conventional architectural practice not be enlarged to encompass a wider vision of human habitation? We would argue, for instance, that the typical core criteria for current housing design of 1) compliance with regulations and recommended standards, 2) financial viability and 3) the veneer of an acceptably modern aesthetic, are likely to be insufficient to create dwellings that can provide the richness, generosity, elegance and emotional support that were regularly afforded by ordinary homes and settlements in the past.

Our focus has been on the home and how it operates, albeit in context, so broader technical issues in city-planning have not been tackled. But research has brought us to the conclusion that there is an important place for high-density low-rise communities near the centre of cities, and that this successful model is applicable globally. We also make a case for housing that recognises the past as well as anticipating the future. We ask of housing that it offer a warm embrace as well as complying with standards. And the economic rationale is made by Yolande Barnes, Head of Research, Savills, for a new kind of family home which is replicable, scaleable, flexible and allied to a change in house-building business models.

The authors and the editor are part of an initiative called Rational House, and this book is an expression of its work and ideas.

1   N J Habraken, The Structure of the Ordinary, MIT Press, 1998, p. 3

CHAPTER 1: THE IDEA OF AN ARCHETYPE

This book is the record of a search to identify the things that appear to have worked well in housing, looking critically at examples of many dwellings, old and new, high rise and low rise, innovative and conventional, in nine world cities. It concludes with a proposal – a model house design, a prototype (Chapter 17) – which represents a synthesis of the best characteristics of housing design from the case studies. By its very nature this concept building is a kind of abstraction which, although it is built in a real street in a real city, could comfortably be placed elsewhere, in another setting, in another city, in the UK or indeed abroad.

The problem of reinvention

It is an unwritten law in today's schools of architecture that students should refrain from looking to the past, and that their work should be entirely original and new. Such an attitude would clearly be unthinkable in other disciplines: imagine a budding chef turning his back on a rich culture of culinary invention from the past, or a young doctor or lawyer being forbidden to research relevant case histories. The tendency to insist on total innovation would be less damaging if confined to the schools, but it is carried over into the practice of everyday architecture and is widely endorsed. Why such a state of mind has arisen is certainly beyond the scope of this book, but what seems apparent is that a line has been drawn in time somewhere in the early 20th century after which a selection of well-designed buildings are considered to exhibit acceptable characteristics, and before which most buildings and the ways they were conceived and constructed are regarded as suspect or irrelevant. As Habraken has observed, 'no sooner had the European intellectual diaspora brought [Walter] Gropius to Harvard (1937) than he reportedly sent the school's premier architectural historian packing'.[1] His was not a lone voice; his belief was widely held across the profession at the time. Gropius's dream, like that of his peers, was that a new architecture should and would 'unlock the door to a shining future in which all building would be radically different from the past, or the war-torn present'.[2] The danger of obliterating an entire history of building, together with all its hard-won lessons (social, personal and technical), seems obvious. But this attitude, one that is obsessively focused on the contemporary while ignoring the past, continues to pervade schools of architecture and the profession.

The paradox of contemporary living

Even the word 'contemporary' has been invested with new meaning. Once merely referring to that which exists at the same time as something else, it is now a word that has come to signify all that is compelling about the present moment, the latest thing, the cutting edge of thought and design. The idea that 'the contemporary' can be represented or reflected or expressed in design may seem exciting. But the notion of designing and creating for a vanishing present only makes sense if the requirements for design are specific to that moment, and the product is disposable. Such criteria are suitable for, say, a news broadcast, or a summer party. But the evolution of human habitation goes far back, so 'the contemporary' can only sensibly be regarded as a small ingredient in a large and well-cultivated requirement set for current housing design.

A quotation from Jan Gehl is apt: 'architects worldwide have increasingly emphasised form. They design weird-looking buildings that resemble perfume bottles and forget to think holistically.'[3]

Figs 1.01, 1.02: Pictograms of the Chair and the House represent recognisable archetypes

Fig. 1.03: Jasper Morrison refines the design of the chair archetype

Notions of archetype: a house is not an airport

Deyan Sudjic examines the concept of established archetypes, those objects that

> have millennia-long histories, with generation after generation producing their own particular interpretations of a given format. These are archetypes that have become so universal as to be invisible, each version building on its predecessors to continually refresh the basic parameters. Who would think of asking who first designed the chair with a leg at each corner?[4]

Like the chair, the house is an ancient archetype, recognisable as a pictogram (Figs 1.01, 1.02).

Such an icon is familiar on our Google search screens, signifying 'home' as a place at the centre of things, a place of return, much more than a 'machine for living' or a survival appliance. These characteristics qualify the house for a different treatment, in design terms, from other forms that we currently see in the built environment. There are now, for example, new buildings that need to accommodate brand new uses, specific to our age: airports, call centres, supermarkets, distribution centres. And these uses need new programmes and new requirement sets. But the house and the settlement qualify for a different treatment. Sudjic has identified a group of product designers, including Jasper Morrison, who are currently returning to archetypes and refining them, and who 'believe that continually inventing new forms is a distraction when there are still so many powerful old ones that still have so much life left in them' (Fig. 1.03).[5] Such an approach, one of refining the archetype, is appropriate, we believe, to the task of housing design.

Future cities

This is not to say that the world of the present does not have its own special challenges. In his portentous book, Hot, Flat, and Crowded,

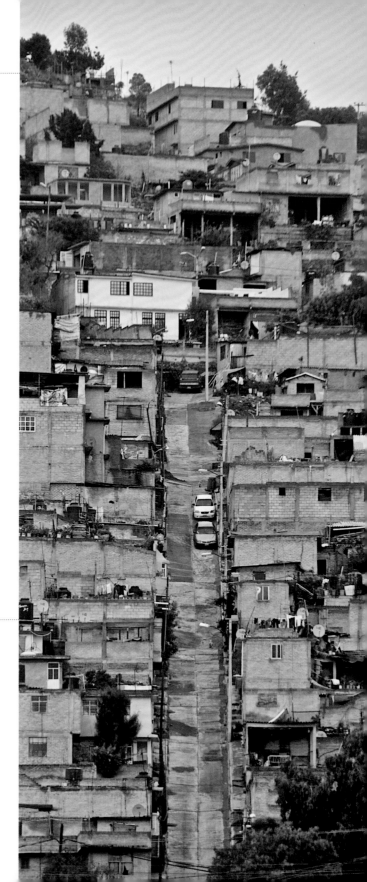

Fig. 1.04: People are migrating to the great cities of the world: the Colonias Populares of Mexico City

Thomas L. Friedman forecasts a future shaped by an exploding population, dwindling resources and irreversible climate change.[6] His 'flat' or democratised world is one in which millions of people are also struggling out of poverty and becoming consumers, both of products and of information. They increasingly have more or less instant awareness of products, markets and news events in distant parts; they are beginning to travel more widely; and, like the rest of us, they are migrating to the great cities of the world (Fig. 1.04).

So any relevant model for 21st-century housing must not only have regard to our rich building heritage, but must also try to anticipate and recognise the seismic changes that are taking place and that will apply new pressures and create new expectations in the future.

The book structure

The book is in three main parts. Part 1 defines and examines 12 key subject areas or parameters for housing, grouped in related pairs:

Density and Urban Form
Flexibility and Adaptability
Appearance and Threshold
Space and Light
Construction and Sustainability
Cost and Value

Methods of evaluating housing are identified and discussed for each of the parameters.

Part 2 presents case studies from nine world cities. For each city there is an overview of its primary historical, economic and social drivers, and the identification of the predominant housing typologies. Six to eight diverse examples are then presented and evaluated using the range of criteria, concepts and metrics developed in Part 1. A more detailed study is provided for at least two of the examples based on an interview with the occupants of the dwelling.

Part 3 tells the story of the creation of a prototype house in west London by Rational House, based on the findings from Parts 1 and 2 of the book. It explains how the concept of the prototype can be extended to form a variety of urban clusters that could provide a framework for successful communities.

The nine world cities

Examples of housing from nine world cities are illustrated in Part 2. More information, expanding the case studies can be found online using the QR icon at the start of Part 2.

The nine cities were selected in three groups of three:

- Three cities that regularly top the charts as providing the most liveable urban environments: Copenhagen, Melbourne and Tokyo.

- Three classic cities with an established, well-recognised and comfortable historic city heritage: London, New York and Paris.

- Three cities that we regarded as more dynamic urban centres that are transforming themselves, or are being transformed, by political, social and economic forces: Berlin, Mexico City and Shanghai.

The choice of cities was representative, if not comprehensive. Nevertheless, housing archetypes such as those opposite were discovered in every city, and this has led to the impression that classic or archetypal dwelling types worthy of study are likely to be present in most major cities. The similarities and differences between the archetypes are revealing and provide valuable lessons (Figs 1.05, 1.06).

Notes to Chapter 1
1   N J Habraken, The Structure of the Ordinary, MIT Press, 1998, p. 269.
2   ibid.
3   Jan Gehl, COWI Magazine (Consultancy Within Engineering, Environmental Science and Economics), October 2010, p. 5.
4   Deyan Sudjic, The Language of Things, Penguin Books, 2008, p. 60.
5   ibid., p. 84.
6   Thomas L. Friedman, Hot, Flat, and Crowded, Penguin Books, 2009.

Figs 1.05, 1.06: Housing archetypes: Kartoffelrækkerne of Copenhagen and Vecindades of Mexico City

PART 1: PARAMETERS

CHAPTER 2: DENSITY AND URBAN FORM

The good city

People are moving to cities (Fig. 2.01). The proportion of people living in conurbations rose dramatically from 13% (220 million) in 1900, to 29% (732 million) in 1950, to 49% (3.2 billion) in 2005.[1] The figure is likely to rise to 60% (4.9 billion) by 2030.[2] And it would be wrong to assume that all of these burgeoning cities are in the developing world. For example, 'on current projections London's population will swell from just under 8 million now to over 9 million by 2031, which is roughly the equivalent of annexing Britain's second city, Birmingham'.[3]

Based on the perception that cities are poised for unlimited growth, the authors of The Endless City have coined the expression 'Urban Age' to describe a coming epoch. 'Cities are the great task of all nation states. They are threatened by scarce resources, environmental problems, new diseases, uncontrolled growth and migration, and by the ethnic and religious conflicts stemming from the despair of disappointed immigrants'.[4] This somewhat dystopian view is one that seems to anticipate inevitable consequences at the end of a path leading from rural equilibrium to urban chaos.

Jonathan Charley, in Writing the Modern City, comments: 'like a fading memory, the pre-capitalist world of villages, churches and fields, of priests, lords and peasants, living a life governed by seasons, tithes and calls to prayer, retreats into the literary hinterland'.[5] This is perhaps a peculiarly English account of the nostalgia for an idyllic past, but every nation will have its own version. Charley is interested in the dichotomy apparent in the writings of novelists and designers about the new metropolis. The works of novelists are 'unimaginable without the modern city's heterotopic estates, slums, mansions, alleys, bars and clubs – the subterranean passages and labyrinths of streets and buildings that make up the "noir" city',[6] while the works of designers reflect 'the enduring belief amongst many architects, urban planners and politicians, that has continued unabated from the urban improvement acts of the nineteenth century, that it is possible through the rational ordering of space to eliminate social disorder and indeed crime'.[7]

Although these are radically different attitudes to the city, both focus on the dark consequences that are perceived to flow from the concentration of population – overcrowding, dereliction, disease, lawlessness – echoing the now distant findings of the Royal Commission on the Housing of the Working Classes, 1885, which equated density with poverty.[8] And of course these ills were the targets of modern movement visionaries such as Le Corbusier with his Plan Voisin for Paris (Fig. 2.02).

There is a third view, however: consider the drawings of Jean-Jacques Sempé of that same city.[9] These are scenes from the recent past, but they could just as easily have been drawn in 1925 when Corb conceived his grand plans (Figs 2.03, 2.04). The Sempé images, however romantic, manage to grasp and to convey the essence of a city of great intensity, opportunity, gaiety, humour and warmth, and above all a city in which there is a place for the individual.

In his important work Good City Form, Kevin Lynch has written of the ill-founded paranoia surrounding the prospect of crowding, and makes the point that

> there have been attempts to connect social pathology with high settlement density, on the premise that an increase in the frequency of stimulus and of encounter, particularly with strangers ... will overload the human capacity to cope, thus bringing on crime, neurosis, stress, ill health and social alienation ... but there is little to show for any effect of residential density.[10]

Fig. 2.01: Megalopolis: Shanghai

Fig. 2.03: Jean-Jacques Sempé: a room in Paris

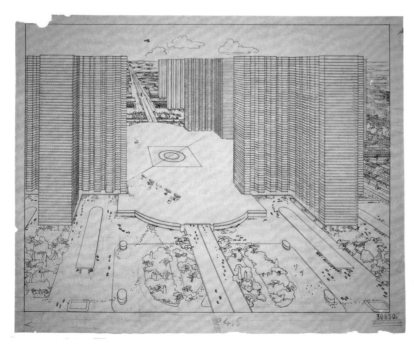

Fig. 2.02: Le Corbusier
Paris, Plan Voisin, 1925
Plan FLC 30850A© FLC

Fig. 2.04: Jean-Jacques Sempé: a balcony overlooking Paris

The great champion of city living, Jane Jacobs, has also painted an entirely different and definitively positive picture. The high-density city is one of immense diversity: of commercial diversity, providing choice, demand, opportunity; of cultural diversity, supporting all manner of ethnic, religious, intellectual and social pursuits; and of diversity in use, full of places to meet, to work in, to celebrate, but also places of safety to withdraw to and relax. She explicitly makes the point that the 'supposed correlation between high densities and trouble, or high densities and slums is simply incorrect'.[11] And further, 'In Brooklyn, New York, the most generally admired, popular and upgrading neighbourhood is Brooklyn Heights; it has much the highest density of dwellings in Brooklyn. Tremendous expanses of failed or decaying Brooklyn gray area have densities half those of Brooklyn Heights or less' (Fig. 2.05).[12]

A newer, influential work in the same vein is Edward Glaeser's book Triumph of the City: How Our Greatest Invention Makes Us Richer, Smarter, Greener, Healthier, and Happier.[13] Not only does the compact city have the potential to be a more enjoyable, richer environment, but it is indisputably a more practical and more sustainable one, reducing, as it does, the time, distance, energy consumption and exhaustion associated with the journeys to places of work, to schools and to shops that we all regularly make. Glaeser points out that 'holding family income and size constant, gas [petrol] consumption per family per year declines by 106 gallons as the number of residents per square mile doubles'.[14]

Beyond all this, the city, as a development format makes economical use of land, our most precious commodity. Intensity of development on city land is an aspiration uniquely shared both by environmentalists and by property developers.

So notwithstanding the many and pressing challenges to provide adequate physical and social support to its expanding corpus, the ever concentrating city is not uniformly evil: indeed, it has the potential to be very good. And there is a growing band

Fig. 2.06: Yesterday's concept of the future: Skyscrapers on Sheikh Zayed Road, Dubai, 2012

Fig. 2.05: High-density living in Brooklyn Heights, New York

of young architects who embrace the charm, the magnetism and the good sense of city living and whose architecture reflects this passion. Stephen Taylor (whose housing work we admire) has said: 'I think at this moment when everyone is addressing the question of sustainability, the idea of making a habitable life in the core or the centre of the city is absolutely the right answer.'[15]

Nevertheless, in the foreword to a more recent edition of her wonderful 'cookbook for the good city', Jane Jacobs bemoans the fact that more than 30 years after it was published planners, architects and developers are still ignoring its wise lessons regarding the shape of neighbourhoods, and are still recreating breathtaking versions of yesterday's concept of the future (Fig. 2.06).

If the megalopolis of Ridley Scott's Blade Runner or Aldous Huxley's Brave New World is to be avoided, then what form is the right form? We have established that high-density living can be desirable (and probably, in the Urban Age, inevitable). Questions immediately arise: what density is the right density and what form should this density take? If we try to answer these questions unequivocally we are again in danger of entering the realm of utopian planning, the vision of an architecture that can heal all ills. But there are, nevertheless, very useful signposts, precedents and lessons that can be observed and that can guide us.

Notions of density

In his very engaging paper entitled Metricity, Paul Clarke introduces us to a wide range of possible density metrics, many of which might give us vivid impressions of what is actually going on in the city.[16] Such measures as languages per hectare, or wireless hotspots per hectare, or health consultants per hectare, or indeed ASBOs per hectare, could provide new clarity to our understanding of urban topography. Unfortunately, such rich information is rarely compiled and we are left, in residential development, with conventional

measures of physical form and of resident population: explicitly, of dwellings per hectare, habitable rooms per hectare and plot ratio.

Of these, the first, dwellings per hectare, is flawed because it does not distinguish between large and small dwellings: a serious deficiency, but this does not prevent the measure being widely used. The second, habitable rooms per hectare, is better because it relates more closely to domestic population density (although not precisely). And the third, plot ratio, is also very useful in helping to infer form and height when site coverage is known.

The measures used in the book for the case-study examples are habitable rooms per hectare (HR/ha), and plot ratio. The following (rough but useful) conversions are helpful in interpreting publicly available data on population and density:

An average net residential population density of, say, 30,000 people per square kilometre = 300 people per hectare = (approx.) 400 HR/ha. A residential density of 400 HR/ha can be achieved with a plot ratio of 1:1 (in other words, a total usable area of floor space equivalent to the total area of the site).

This residential density (400 HR/ha) and this plot ratio (1:1) are approximately equivalent, for example, to the density achieved by a 90-square-metre two-storey terraced house on an 18-metre-deep plot with small back and front garden, of a type pervasive across London.

As points of reference, the invaluable GLA handbook Housing for a Compact City (2003)[17] quoted the then Draft London Plan's recommended densities of 200–450 HR/ha for houses with car parking in urban areas and 450–700 HR/ha for houses and/or flats with car parking in central areas. Jane Jacobs goes further, and suggests an ideal minimum density for central areas of 100 dwellings per acre (or very approximately 750 HR/ha).[18]

The relationship between density and form

Housing for a Compact City was a guide initiated by the then mayor, Ken Livingstone, and written by the architect Richard Rogers. It makes the case that a sustainable future for London depends on the creation of a compact (dense), mixed-use city.

The diagram overleaf from the handbook explores graphically the relationships between height, density and plot ratio (Fig. 2.07).[19] It shows how different forms of architecture, including a terraced street layout, a series of four-storey flat blocks and a single high-rise building, all at a density of 75 small dwellings per hectare, or, say, 300 HR/ha, can be accommodated on the same plot and at the same plot ratio (of approximately 0.75:1).

The book also provides many very clear and sometimes surprising examples of the relative densities achieved by a variety of building forms. For example, the pioneering development of flats in Churchill Gardens (master-planned in 1952), consisting of blocks of between 6 and 11 storeys, yields a density of 557 HR/ha. This is a respectable inner-city density but it is achieved at the expense of the loss of any street life, exchanged for anonymous open space. By contrast, the six-storey terraced blocks in Linden Gardens, Notting Hill, are said to achieve a remarkable density of 1000 HR/ha – almost twice as much – and here the features of the grander 19th-century terraces, gracious streets and squares are wonderfully preserved, with no sense of overcrowding (Fig. 2.08).

Another striking comparison can be made between the seven-storey Haussmann flat blocks in Sempé's charming drawings (which yield densities in excess of 1200 HR/ha and plot ratios of over 3:1, similar to our archetype from Paris), and London's Alton Estate blocks in Roehampton, arguably a realisation on a significant scale of Le Corbusier's early vision for the city. Here the density is only about 400 HR/ha (see Chapter 11, Case study 1).

And one of the most telling examples from our travels comes from Shanghai. Here we were advised by a local (European) estate agent that we should, without fail, visit a newly completed residential development called Top of City, 15 minutes' walk from People's Square. In 2003, Mayor Han Zheng established a density limit on new city-centre housing based on a plot ratio of 2.5:1, a standard to which this development complied (Fig. 2.09).

But although slick, the private estate had all the hallmarks of Le Corbusier's (1920s') vision and it was sterile, set in manicured gardens that no one used, devoid of street life, forbidding in spite of the high standards of finish and attention to detail. Not far away, however, we encountered one of the many splendid districts of Lilong, or lane houses (see Chapter 16), full of life and colour, and a favourite hang-out area for local office workers in their lunch hour. This wonderful city quarter was built in the 1930s, to the same plot ratio of 2.5:1 (or density of approximately 1000 HR/ha) (Fig. 2.10).

The perception that high residential density is synonymous with multi-storey flat blocks persists and recurs. Another interesting example is the splendidly intense development in Spitterlauer Lande, Vienna, by Zaha Hadid. Notwithstanding its impressive form, this achieves a density of less than 250 HR/ha (Fig. 2.11).

The fact is that this notion, connecting height with density, was dispelled well before Richard Rogers's GLA report published in 2003. Studies by Leslie Martin and Lionel March at Cambridge in the 1960s demonstrated that courtyard housing could provide (an astonishing) five times more accommodation than point-block developments on an equivalent site,[20] and such low-rise densities were subsequently realised in new schemes by Neyland and Unglass, and by Phippen Randall and Parkes (now PRP) (Fig. 2.12).

Problems with high-rise living

So when considering the high-density city, we appear to have choices in design about whether to go high or low. High rise was

Clockwise from bottom left:

Fig. 2.07: Three urban forms giving the same density: Housing for a Compact City

Fig. 2.08: Linden Gardens, London: 1,000 habitable rooms per hectare

Fig. 2.09: Top of City, Shanghai: 1,000 habitable rooms per hectare

Fig. 2.10: Typical Lilong, Shanghai: 1,000 habitable rooms per hectare

intended to create urban-scale densities in a garden setting. But the evident failures of the aspirational towers of the postwar period are well documented.[21] Jan Gehl, in Life Between Buildings, laments:

> The functionalists made no mention of the psychological and social aspects of the design of buildings or public spaces. That building design could influence play activities, contact patterns, and meeting possibilities was not considered. One of the most noticeable effects of this ideology was that streets and squares disappeared from the new building projects and the new cities.[22]

Our own conclusions regarding high-rise residential development, based on interviews and examples in a number of our nine cities, are recorded in subsequent chapters, but can be summarised as follows:

High rise

- Is more expensive to build and to maintain
- Consumes more energy in use
- Is less successful in providing the right conditions for a sense of community
- Generally fails to provide an attractive and vibrant form at street level, and separates residents from street life
- Creates ambiguous intermediate space between the public street and the private front door
- Cannot be easily adapted to other uses
- Provides inadequate outside private amenity space

Fig. 2.11: Flats in Vienna by Zaha Hadid: 250 habitable rooms per hectare

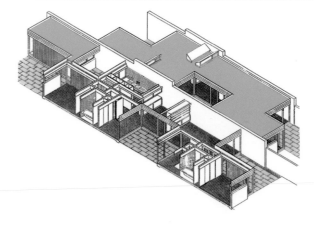

Fig. 2.12: The Ryde, Hatfield, by PRP: early high-density low-rise living

And finally, one of the headline problems with high-rise flat blocks is that you cannot, in our view, make good cities out of them. Looking out over Paris from a flat on the top floor of a 32-storey block can be exhilarating, but only because one is looking out over Paris. When the view is dominated by similar creations (as it is in parts of Shanghai, for instance) the effect is exactly the opposite.

What form of high-density low rise?

The principle that high-density low rise can be achieved has been demonstrated with some modern examples, but we were, of course, interested to analyse and compare the best of the examples we found in our own research.

Below is a table of the densities achieved by each of our nine city archetypes:

APPROXIMATE AVERAGE FOR TYPE		HR/ha	Plot ratio
Copenhagen:	Kartoffelraekkerne (Potato Rows)	500	1.25:1
Melbourne:	Victorian terraces	600	1.5:1
Toyko:	Mini-houses	600	1.5:1
London:	Georgian houses	800	2.0:1
New York:	Brownstone houses	1000	2.5:1
Paris:	Post-Haussmann flat blocks	1200	3.0:1
Berlin:	Altbau	1200	3.0:1
Mexico City:	Vecindades	700	1.75:1
Shanghai:	Shikumen and lane housing	1000	2.5:1

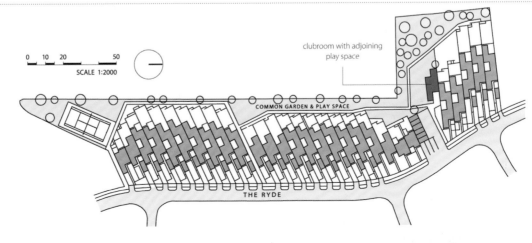

0 10 20   50
SCALE 1:2000

clubroom with adjoining play space

COMMON GARDEN & PLAY SPACE

THE RYDE

Fig. 2.13a: The right balance of compactness, relationship with street and adaptability: west London Victorian terraces

Very interesting comparisons can be made between the above cases and the many specific examples given in the excellent reference volume D Book: Density, Data, Diagrams, Dwellings by Aurora Fernandez Per, Javier Mozas and Javier Arpa.[23] District and city-wide (gross) densities, as well as plot densities, are given for each example. The point that becomes clear in making these comparisons is that the densities of the classic forms (above) regularly match those achieved by recently built multi-storey flat blocks, except in the most dense central and business districts of cities.

Conclusions

For us, the best housing was that which presented the right balance of compactness (high density) and relationship with street, provided modest private open space and could be adapted to other uses (Figs. 2.13a and b). All of these attributes relate to form and density. And these conclusions are not, as we discover, strikingly unique, but are shared with others, including those involved in the movement known as New Urbanism.

Looking at the archetypes for each city (table above), we concluded that a relatively high density of about 800 HR/ha (plot ratio 2:1) was achievable without recourse to a point-block format. For our case-study evaluations, we worked on the basis that a density for low-rise development of about 450 HR/ha or greater was very desirable.

In observing what appears to work as a good relationship between density and form, in this chapter we are avoiding, for the moment, considerations of cost and value (particularly site value) and the effects these factors will have. Such matters are explored in Chapter 7.

Notes to Chapter 2

1   The Revision of the UN World Urbanization Prospects Report (2005), United Nations publication, 2006, p.1.
2   ibid.
3   'The changing face of London', The Economist, 28 January–3 February 2012, p. 23.
4   Wolfgang Nowak, foreword in, Ricky Burdett, Deyan Sudjic, The Endless City, Phaidon Press, 2007, p. 7.
5   Jonathan Charley, 'Time, space and narrative', in Writing the Modern City, Routledge, 2012, p. 3.
6   ibid., p. 12.
7   ibid., p. 13.
8   Report of the Royal Commission on the Housing of the Working Classes, British Central Government, 1885.
9   Jean-Jacques Sempé, Un peu de Paris, Editions Gallimard, 2001.

10 Kevin Lynch, Good City Form, MIT Press, 1984, p. 263.
11 Jane Jacobs, The Death and Life of Great American Cities, Random House, 1993, p. 263.
12 ibid., p. 264.
13 Edward Glaeser, Triumph of the City: How Our Greatest Invention Makes Us Richer, Smarter, Greener, Healthier, and Happier, Macmillan Publishers, 2011.
14 ibid., p.207.
15 Stephen Taylor and Ryue Nishizawa, Some Ideas on Living in London and Tokyo, Canadian Centre for Architecture, Lars Muller Publishers, 2008, p. 117.
16 Paul Clarke, Metricity: Exploring New Measures of Urban Density, Royal College of Art, Helen Hamlyn Centre, 2006.
17 Richard Rogers, Housing for a Compact City, Greater London Authority, 2003.
18 Jacobs, op. cit., p. 276.
19 Rogers, op. cit., p. 20.
20 Leslie Martin and Lionel March, Urban Space and Structures, Cambridge University Press, 1972, pp. 36–7.
21 Alice Coleman, Utopia on Trial, Vision and Reality in Planned Housing, H. Shipman, 1985.
22 Jan Gehl, Life Between Buildings: Using Public Space, Island Press, 2011, p. 45.
23 Aurora Fernandez Per, Javier Mozas and Javier Arpa, D Book: Density, Data, Diagrams, Dwellings, Vitoria-Gasteiz, 2007.

Fig. 2.13b: Point blocks make dysfunctional communities: outer ring of central Shanghai

CHAPTER 3: FLEXIBILITY AND ADAPTABILITY

What is meant by 'flexible' and 'adaptable'?

These words are often used imprecisely, and sometimes interchangeably, so it is worth clarifying what they are intended to mean in this chapter. Where we live in London, we are surrounded by older dwellings that have been interpreted in a variety of ways over time, often accommodating a succession of family groupings differentiated by, for example, size, age, income and culture. In some cases, buildings have also been transformed from one use to another: from residences, to offices, sometimes to retail space and restaurants, and even back to residential use. London is by no means unique in possessing such clever structures. In fact, they are not uncommon in larger cities everywhere (Figs. 3.01a and b).

Broadly, we see two kinds of change:

There are internal alterations and additions to dwellings created to express and accommodate different patterns of life. The ability to easily accept these changes, we call flexibility.

And there are wholesale changes of use, which could reflect an evolving urban or commercial context. The ability to respond to these influences, we call adaptability.

These are working definitions that, although not perfect, allow us to distinguish between the response to a need for changes of format largely within the dwelling, resulting in physical alteration (flexibility), and the response to a need for a comprehensive reinterpretation of space, possibly for a different use, without the need for radical physical change in the primary structure (adaptability).

It would seem to be self-evident that high levels of flexibility and adaptability are very desirable. Particularly now, when sustainability is high on the agenda, buildings that can be interpreted in a variety of ways, enabling an extension to their useful lives, become more durable and better-performing assets, as well as giving their occupants greater choice. But the requirement for these features rarely appears in architectural briefs. Perhaps this reflects the short-term concerns of many developers and volume house builders. Notwithstanding the present shortage of good and long-lasting housing, it seems that little is being done to avoid rigidity and the potential for redundancy and obsolescence in the design of current housing product.

Indeed there is positive encouragement to identify, for example, the differentiators between tenants of affordable housing and owner-occupiers, effectively precluding flexible and mixed-tenure arrangements. Among these, for instance, is the evident need for properly ventilated bedrooms for teenagers in the affordable category who will spend a lot of time there, in contrast to the open-plan living style allegedly preferred by their more affluent counterparts; and the need for sunlit private open space for affordable tenants, who, unlike the owner-occupiers cannot afford to spend time in the sunshine abroad.[1]

Notwithstanding the absence of focus on these issues in practice, the theoretical case for flexibility and adaptability is well made in a number of recent books, notably Tools for Inhabiting the Present, by Josep Montaner, Zaida Muxi and David Falagan,[2] and Flexible Housing, by Jeremy Till and Tatjana Schneider.[3] In both cases, the authors are, unusually, prepared to analyse projects and evaluate their effectiveness, rather than simply showcasing a selection of current work.

Till is particularly clear about the connotations often misapplied to the word 'flexibility':

There is a simplistic association of flexibility with progress: something that can move escapes the shackles of tradition,

Fig. 3.01a: Mixing other uses with residential: Copenhagen, Mexico City

Fig. 3.01b: Mixing other uses with residential: Shanghai

something that can be changed is forever new. To this extent flexibility, read literally, provides a convenient and immediate fix to that common architectural need to be allied to the 'progressive' forces of modernity. It is therefore not surprising that the received history of flexibility in architecture is dominated by a list of seminal, one-off, experiments that play directly with the rhetoric of flexibility: buildings with parts that actually move (Rietveld's Schroder Huis, Le Corbusier's Maisons Loucheur and Chareau's Maison de Verre set the pace in the 1920s).[4]

The Maisons Loucheur concept was conceived as flexible housing that featured movable and fold-down furniture elements. Designed in 1928/9, it followed from Corb's early Maison Domino drawings (1914) and also from the buildings he designed for the Weissenhofsiedlung in Stuttgart (1927). All three sprang from the same root idea, expressed in the diagram (below left) which appeared in Precisions in 1930 (Fig 3.02).

Here, a stark contrast is drawn between a framed structure allowing free elevations and floor plans, and a loadbearing equivalent, evidently compromised by its form of construction. But Le Corbusier's fascination with the plastic and aesthetic capabilities of the concrete frame have, it would appear, encouraged him to suggest a false dichotomy where flexibility is concerned: with a few simple alterations to the diagram, a modified loadbearing structure (below right, Fig 3.03) appears to afford all the functional freedom available from the frame solution, but also allows more opportunity for subdivision and recombination of spaces, provides better access to the street, achieves a higher density and provides the opportunity for better urban integration than the Corb model.

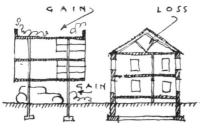

Fig 3.02: Le Corbusier
Les 5 points d'une architecture nouvelle, 1926
Extrait de l'Œuvre Complète vol1, 1910-1929, p.129

Fig 3.03: Is a load bearing structure
less flexible than a frame?

Till explains that the modern movement icons of flexibility generally failed to deliver in practice, noting that 'it is the actuality of these latter buildings, those that provide a literal image of flexibility, that is most telling: once built their parts remained fixed in place' (Fig 3.04).[5]

How are flexibility and adaptability achieved?

Even if the above well-known examples were unsuccessful as repeatable models, the search for designs that foster adaptability and flexibility is a worthwhile one, so books like those by Till and Montaner are valuable sources. To summarise, the principal features that appear to promote these qualities, identified by the authors, are:

Absence of a hierarchy in the main rooms:
This is also known as indeterminacy, or polyvalency, and it refers to the characteristic that the rooms are of a size, shape and location such that they can be used for a variety of purposes; and that those purposes can change over cycles of time ranging from a single day to the lifetime of the building. Room naming is therefore absent, since any of the principal spaces can be designated as a living room or a family room, or bedroom, or even a kitchen/dining space (depending on the servicing arrangements).

Absence of obstructive loadbearing internal walls and partitions:
Clear spans obviously allow multiple configurations of larger spaces, facilitating easy aggregation and subdivision of rooms to suit any occupier. The presence of simple and level ceilings and floor surfaces also enhances this freedom.

Fig. 3.04: Rietveld Schröder House: the image of flexibility, designed by Gerrit Th. Rietveld, 1924 – The Rietveld Schröder House is part of the Centraal Museum, Utrecht

Fig. 3.05: Permeability: Cottage, Walton-on-Thames

Key:

A Hall
B Scullery
C Kitchen
D Room

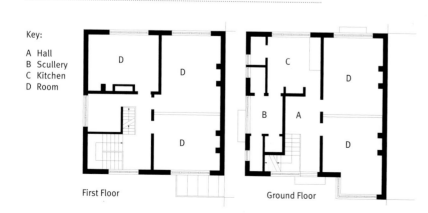

First Floor   Ground Floor

Regularity of the facade:

A building facade composed of windows of similar size, large enough to provide adequate light for any use, placed at intervals that anticipate possible subdivision, will increase the freedom provided by a flexible plan. The practice of constructing regular elevations is universally followed in, for instance, commercial office design, where the need to reconfigure floor space very easily and repeatedly is perhaps more obvious.

Ease of adding to, changing or updating services:

The presence of vertical mains plumbing and waste services in more than one location on any floor plate will clearly allow the creation of a bathroom and/or kitchen in one of two locations on any floor. The assumption that the positions of these facilities can be fixed for the life of the building fabric is obviously wrong, on the simple observation of transformations that are evident in older buildings all around us. Clearly, these alterations can be made easier by anticipating change at the outset of design. The other services – electrical, ventilation, security, fire safety and communication – are likely to require more dramatic alterations with each change of use, so the provision of zones in which these can be located and relocated flexibly is very beneficial.

Permeability of the circulation:

One of the early case studies in Till's book is a modest cottage in Walton-on-Thames (Fig. 3.05).[6] It is conceived as a family house, but each of the five principal rooms is what he refers to as 'generic': in other words, of a size and orientation that can be used for any

purpose. And crucially, the staircase is placed at the front of the building, so that each generic room on both floors can be accessed directly from it. This simple arrangement means that the building can be, and indeed has been, subdivided into apartments with relative ease. It is unnecessary to go through any living space to get to a staircase. This dis-association of the circulation greatly benefits both flexibility and adaptability.

Ease of extension:

The ability of a family to extend space rather than move to another location has evident cost, time and sustainability benefits. Where building plots permit, small back extensions are ubiquitous. Loft and basement conversions within the building outline are also extremely popular. Till introduces a further idea, using the expression 'slack space' to describe areas within the building plan – such as courtyards, enlarged stairwells, alcoves and areas of flat roof – that can be appropriated into the home, post occupation.[7] A famous example would be Herman Hertzberger's Diagoon Houses, where substantial slack space has been incorporated at the outset (Fig. 3.06).[8]

All of the above are in the nature of what Till calls 'soft' measures, features that allow the user to decide the form of adaptation he or she requires. They are distinguished from 'hard' measures, which are the techniques predetermined by a designer to achieve a particular result, such as sliding or movable partitions, or fold-down furniture. And it is the latter features which have proved to be less successful, and the former which have really worked. Stewart

Fig. 3.06: Slack Space: Diagoon Housing, Delft (1967–70) by Architectuurstudio HH, architect Herman Hertzberger.

Key:

A Garage
B Hall
C Slack space
D Living
E Kitchen
F Dining
G Bedroom

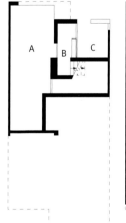

Ground Floor

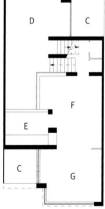

First Floor

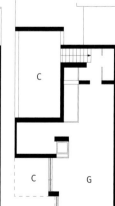

Second Floor

Brand's often quoted but incomplete syllogism 'all buildings are predictions; all predictions are wrong' suggests that we should try harder to understand the benefits of soft measures, lest our buildings become obsolete.[9]

The term 'perfectibility' has also been used by architect Ignacio Paricio (Universitat Politecnica de Catalunya) to summarise the benefits of applying all the so-called soft measures together. Resulting structures can be interpreted in diverse ways to suit their inhabitants.

Fig 3.07: Borneo Sporenburg development, Amsterdam: responsive but not flexible

What is the role of consultation?

If perfectibility, by each successive occupant, is a realistic goal in a dwelling that has many soft measures, then what is the standing of the ideas of Habraken and others who have suggested that the answer to consumer choice lies not in loose-fit flexibility but in the practice of consultation? They promote the notion of a building framework in which individual modules are completed on the basis of customised design, facilitated by a consultative team on behalf of each of the initial owners.[10] The most widely publicised expression of this idea is the Borneo development, part of the regeneration of Amsterdam's eastern docks (Fig 3.07). A piece of the island was subdivided into 60 individual freehold plots, and the new owners with their architects were encouraged to design bespoke houses conforming to a limited number of principles, such as plot size and building height. This is a wonderfully diverse project, but it does not actually address the question of long-term flexibility and adaptability because each individual dwelling is unique and will be constrained by its functional and structural specificity.

The same reservation could be expressed about the attempts at housing mass customisation, such as the choice-based sales

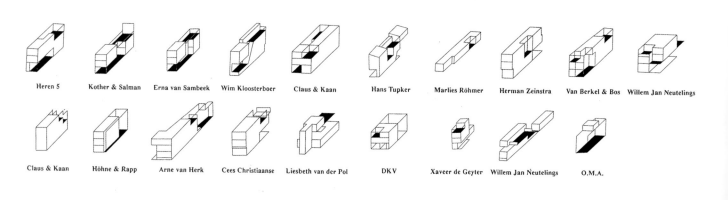

Heren 5   Kother & Salman   Erna van Sambeek   Wim Kloosterboer   Claus & Kaan   Hans Tupker   Marlies Röhmer   Herman Zeinstra   Van Berkel & Bos   Willem Jan Neutelings

Claus & Kaan   Höhne & Rapp   Arne van Herk   Cees Christiaanse   Liesbeth van der Pol   DKV   Xaveer de Geyter   Willem Jan Neutelings   O.M.A.

system advanced by London architects HTA. This model allows the purchaser to make selections in design using a web-based interface. The resulting dwellings, while tailor-made for the initial owners, are unlikely to be perfect for subsequent occupants, and will be too specific to enable wholesale changes to mixed uses.

Some examples of flexibility and adaptability

We encountered many impressive examples of the alterations and adaptations facilitated by modest low-rise buildings.

Denmark has its classic Kartoffelraekkerne or 'Potato Rows', originally workers' cottages, now much sought-after family homes, near the city centre. Each interior is now different, but the simple 'bones' of the terraces remain and give these streets great coherence and simplicity. At junctions with the adjoining busier streets, the ground floors have been converted to shops (see Chapter 8).

In Brooklyn, the classic brownstone can easily be configured as flats or stacked maisonettes. And in Queens, a modest two-up/two-down has been subdivided vertically rather than horizontally, to form two dwellings back to back. These made tiny flats, each with an entrance from ground level, but the owners had the option to reconnect the two parts to make a larger house as their family grew (see Chapter 12).

The Lilong structures of Shanghai provide a wonderful counter-form to the vibrant, chaotic and ever-changing lifestyle that thrives there. They have served many purposes since their construction in the early 20th century (see Chapter 16).

In Mexico City, there are a variety of traditional vecindades, all similar in structure and all very different in the way they have been interpreted. One of them had even been converted into a music school (see Chapter 15) (Fig 3.08).

In central Melbourne, we looked at a terrace of what had been five identical Victorian houses. We interviewed a family whose house had been completely reconfigured as a generous live-work home, with private space for the teenage children and an internal courtyard. Next door was an unconverted house, used by an older couple; to the other side, a house that was being used as a psychiatrist's office; and next to that, two houses which had been joined together to make a convent and refuge (see Chapter 9) (Fig. 3.09).

In London, we saw that mews houses were easily transformed to serve the requirements of countless different family structures and needs but could also be adapted to serve as offices, gymnasia,

Fig 3.08: Vecindad, Mexico City: housing terrace converted to music school

Fig 3.09: Melbourne Victorian: family homes, a refuge for women and psychiatrist's offices in one terrace

Fig. 3.10: Edinburgh New Town: real flexibility behind composed street facades

workshops and studios. And here we also have the redoubtable Georgian house, whose simple structure has lent itself to a similarly varied, if more formal, range of uses (see Chapter 11).

Georgian houses are of course not confined to London, and there are examples of these unusually fine buildings across the UK. Michael Carley writes of the terraced housing which replaced densely packed tenement buildings in Edinburgh's fortified Old Town between 1765 and1850:

> Within the conception of wide streets, garden squares and unified neo-classical facades, there is an enormous variety of housing available behind the New Town's inscrutable fan-lit Georgian front doors from one-room studios to five-bedroom flats. The only clue to this variation is that some doors have one doorbell and others may have eight, ten or even sixteen, depending on the number of flats accessible from the communal staircase. The social implication is a lively mix of families with children, singles and childless couples, retired people and flat sharers of all sorts including students; genuinely a 'mixed income, mixed use' community of great elegance.

This wonderful example of flexible planning deserves another entire book of description and analysis (Fig. 3.10).11

Summary

In general, we have found that generic and simple structures of two to five storeys in height, with modest clear spans of 4 to 5 metres, and with staircases positioned to allow permeability, are the most flexible. They prove also to be the most adaptable to other uses – including commercial space for selling, eating and working – when found at busy corners or at other points of transition between more public and more private thoroughfares.

Highly flexible and adaptable buildings not only serve their occupants well, by providing space which can be adjusted to changing needs and dispositions, but also benefit the larger community. Buildings which last longer, and which can accept many interpretations, ultimately make more cost-effective use of materials and energy, and in so doing they clearly help to create an urban environment that is more robust and more sustainable.

Notes to Chapter 3

1   David Levitt, The Housing Design Handbook, Routledge, 2010, p. 163.

2   Josep Montaner, Zaida Muxi and David Falagan, Tools for Inhabiting the Present: Housing in the 21st Century, Universitat Politecnica de Catalunya, 2011.

3   Jeremy Till and Tatjana Schneider, Flexible Housing, Architectural Press, 2007.

4   ibid., p. 5.

5   ibid., p. 6.

6   ibid., p. 56.

7   ibid., p. 185.

8   ibid., p. 82.

9   Stewart Brand, How Buildings Learn, Penguin, 1994, p. 178.

10   N J Habraken, Support: An Alternative to Mass Housing, English Edition, Architectural Press, 1972.

11   Michael Carley, retired Professor of the Built Environment at Heriot-Watt University, Edinburgh.

CHAPTER 4: APPEARANCE AND THRESHOLD

In this chapter, we consider two aspects of the visual impact of homes: the way they look from the outside, and the way they create a transition from the public world outside the home to the private world within.

Beauty

In thinking about the appearance of buildings, we immediately confront the thorny issue of aesthetics: questions of the nature of beauty and ugliness, and whether there can be any kind of agreement on these perceptions. Debate on the subject has played out for centuries, so it would be pointless to attempt a definitive summing-up in this slim volume. Indeed, it is difficult to talk about the subject at all, but this is unfortunate since the appearance of buildings and their emotional impacts are very important to most of us. We all have strong views about the cities we have loved and hated, and about the streets and buildings of which they are made. And the importance of beauty is something we all recognise. In the words of Richard Jefferies, the 19th-century English writer, 'the hours we are absorbed by beauty are the only hours when we really live … This is real life, and all else is illusion, or mere endurance.'[1]

The appeal of cities, and the buildings of cities, is stimulated by an awareness of complexity, opportunity and the prospect of excitement, as well as a reading of the urban environment in purely visual terms. And layers of knowledge and association tend, of course, to individualise the perception of a particular environment. So, even putting aside the problem of subjectivity in aesthetics, a discussion of the emotional impact of the appearance of buildings is a challenging and multifaceted one.

Fig. 4.01: Typical 'First Rate' Georgian, showing proportioning principles (after Cruickshank)

Fig. 4.02: The Blue House by FAT, 2002, London

Fig. 4.03: The ideal city, 1470, Piero della Francesca: a study in good scale and good proportions?

But if we take, for example, the Georgian house, perhaps universally accepted as an attractive object, and also very successful as a building block for city space, for terraces, streets and squares, and if we try to describe the characteristics that make it beautiful, we may have a starting point (Fig. 4.01).

Character

The notion of 'character' is often applied as a test for housing quality. In 2001, CABE (Commission for Architecture and the Built Environment) advanced a tool to assess compliance with quality standards for projects being considered for public sector funding, called Building For Life. This included a series of five questions intended to establish whether or not a scheme displayed character, first among which was the question: 'Is the design specific to the scheme?'

Do we consider that Georgian houses have character? We think the answer would generally be yes. But given that the type can be found in all parts of the UK from Edinburgh to Bath and beyond, is it not a dwelling form that actually represents the antithesis of the CABE criterion? It is a design which is anything but specific to its scheme (or location). Perhaps CABE's requirement for uniqueness as a condition for 'character' arises from a contemporary architectural culture, one which encourages or assumes individual expression and which seeks solutions that are strongly influenced by site-specific conditions (and both of these are 20th-century design inclinations).

So if the notion of 'character' is not easy to pin down, what then are the less ambiguous attributes that could describe the special appeal of Georgian houses? Our list would include authenticity, good scale, good proportions, economy of means and identity.

Authenticity

Buildings that express the technical and social circumstances in which they are constructed are visually and intellectually satisfying. This is a proposition that applies as well to Elizabethan or ancient Greek buildings as it does to buildings constructed in the 21st century. The corollary is that buildings recreating or imitating the appearance of details from the past, using today's methods, have a faux quality that transports us (intentionally or otherwise) out of the real world and into a kind of cartoon realm of irony, or kitsch or pastiche (Fig. 4.02).

Georgian homes were typically fashioned from the clay on which they stood and were built to high densities, in a manner that would now be regarded as highly sustainable. Although pure

imitation of historic models does not work, an understanding of the underlying principles of design from any period can be valuable – and the Georgian model has unusual relevance for the design of city living today.

Good scale

The question arises as to what is the best height, and the best form, for housing judged in purely visual terms (Fig. 4.03). Georgian terraces of three or four storeys are indeed universally admired. The pressures and dependencies associated with height, density, cost and value are explored in Chapter 7. These often determine what can actually be built at a particular location in the city. But when there is choice, what is the optimum form taking into account density and height? In his book A Pattern Language, Christopher Alexander writes:

> High buildings have no genuine advantages, except in speculative gains ... They are not cheaper, they destroy townscape, they destroy social life, they promote crime, they make life difficult for children, they are expensive to maintain, they wreck the open spaces near them and they damage light and air and view.[2]

He goes on to provide research references to support these claims.

An environment constructed entirely of such blocks would be a disaster, both in terms of the outlook from flats and also at street level. Such a nightmare has actually been made real, as we have seen in parts of Shanghai.

Good proportions

Much is said of the beauty of Georgian proportions, as if they possessed a kind of magic. But the principles behind them, using square construction modules of 3 feet 6 inches to determine

window widths, and the horizontal and vertical distances between facade elements, are actually very simple, as recorded by Dan Cruickshank (Fig. 4.01).[3]

There are other proportioning systems, of course, notably the golden rectangle or divine proportion. Much is claimed for this system and its resonance with natural geometries, and it has been used by architects and builders both ancient and modern.[4] A golden rectangle can (uniquely) be cut into a square and a smaller rectangle with the same aspect ratio as the enclosing rectangle (Fig 4.05).

The application of such a proportioning tool shares with the Georgian system a set of clear geometric relationships between the visually well-defined elements of the structure, both among themselves and in relation to the whole.

Such relationships could be described as 'consonance'. This consonance is not an abstract idea: it is visible. An analogy with music can be drawn here. Most music is built on scales and intervals of consonant frequencies, which are easily discernible. When composers deviate from consonance they create tension which, in their compositions, is resolved by returning in stages to consonance. The intentional use of dissonance in music is a kind of sophistication: the greater the dissonance, the more sophisticated (and smaller) is the audience. Indeed, it is no exaggeration to say that all popular music is built firmly on consonant harmonies. So it is, dare we say, in architecture. An environment full of irregularity and arbitrary geometry controlled by no natural or conceived order may be a diverting spectacle, but it is perceived as a deviation from consonance, and at its extreme it is merely incoherent. Georgian housing is visually coherent.

Economy of means

The use of everyday materials, organised in pleasing proportions, with windows providing plentiful natural light appropriate to the

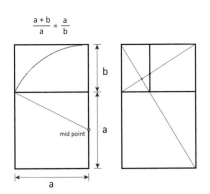

$$\frac{a + b}{a} = \frac{a}{b}$$

b

a

mid point

a

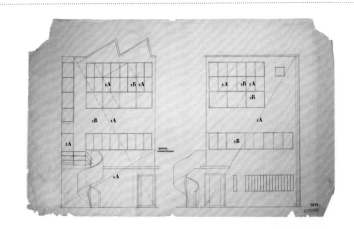

Fig 4.05a (far left)
Golden Rectangle:
construction

Fig 4.05b (left)
Golden Rectangle:
proportion

Fig 4.05c (right)
Golden Rectangle:
application
Le Corbusier
Paris
Maison-atelier Ozenfant,
1922
Plan FLC 7850 © FLC:

rooms they serve, has yielded what has been called 'elegance' in the case of Georgian house-building. This is not gentility but a kind of simplicity, as in the elegance prized by scientists: a simple solution that solves multiple problems at once in the most economical way.

Identity

We found that the expression of identity in the outside appearance of a home varied inversely with density. In the most dense examples – high-rise flats in, say, New York or Paris or Shanghai – occupants were neither easily able nor very interested to identify their personal cell from the street, and their sense of the appearance of their place of residence was bound up in an impression of the building as a whole, and of the neighbourhood in which it was located. At the

other extreme, in the cases of suburban houses at Levittown, New York, or on the outskirts of Melbourne, every effort has been made to distinguish the entire building from its neighbours, by colour, by extensions, by re-cladding and by changing of roof shapes. This tendency is particularly striking at Levittown, where most of the original single-storey houses, constructed to an identical design in the 1940s, had been completely transformed (Fig. 4.06).

Terraced houses fall somewhere between the two extremes, sometimes exhibiting changes of colour but often relying only on the unique features of the main entrance to convey distinction. This is the case with Georgian houses, as explained by Cruickshank: 'No matter how economical the structure, nor how austere the design, it was practically inevitable that at least a little extravagance and a little freedom of design would be allowed for the door' (Fig. 4.07).[5] What is interesting is that this house format, while it is

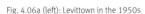
Fig. 4.06a (left): Levittown in the 1950s

Fig. 4.06b (right): Levittown, New York: every house is now different

Fig. 4.07: Georgian houses in Armagh: identity and civitas

read in terraces as part of the city fabric, also allows just enough freedom of personal expression at the most important point of public exposure. So it permits the expression of an identity without completely dissociating the dwelling from the public arena (as is the case at Levittown).

Threshold

We found that this point of transition, the threshold, worked in a variety of ways in our case studies, some more successful than others. For instance, we looked at several very similar terraced housing communities in Copenhagen, and noted that the use of space in front of the house, and the amount of interaction with neighbours that this encouraged, seemed to be related to the number of steps at the front entrance. Families in houses with a flush threshold tended to use their forecourts more freely than did those who entered their houses from one or two steps.

Entrances approached by significant staircases, such as those of the New York brownstones, were even more detached and formal in character. As is the case with Georgian houses, the brownstones often have lower-ground floors with a resulting light well or courtyard spaces up to the pavement, creating a bridge effect to mark the passage from outside to inside.

The requirement for detachment is naturally more evident on busier streets. In these cases, gates, porches and recessed entrances helped to reduce the sense of abrupt change between street activities and the tranquillity of interior space. Such devices create the 'soft edges' that Jan Gehl advocates in Life Between Buildings, spaces that not only afford a comfortable transition but also create places to linger (see Chapter 9, Case study 1).[6]

In cases where thresholds were flush, and where the street itself was used as an extension of the house – as with the Lilong houses in Shanghai, the best of the Kartoffelraekkerne in Copenhagen and

Fig. 4.09: Roupell Street, 1820, London: quiet houses

Fig. 4.08: Lilong houses, Shanghai: five levels of hierarchy to reach the interior

the mews houses of London – detachment was created by a clear hierarchy of streets going from busy/very public/dominated by cars, to quiet/semi-public/car-tolerant, so that by the time the individual entrance was reached the space immediately in front of it was no longer regarded as entirely in the public realm. In some cases, such as the Lilong houses, there could be as many as five levels of hierarchy before the interior was reached: busy thoroughfare/side street/lane/courtyard/entrance. (Fig. 4.08)

The experience of threshold for dwellers of multistorey flats is altogether different. While their sense of detachment is ensured, it is achieved at a cost. They are withdrawn completely from the life of the street, and homes are often approached through a sequence of anonymous lobbies, staircases or lift cars and corridors before they are eventually reached.

Quietness

When considering, above, whether 'character' could be defined we mentioned the modern movement presumption that each example of good housing should display some striking originality. And yet one of the most successful examples, the Georgian house, is characterised by repetition and regularity. We found similar attributes in the case-study examples that scored highest in our assessments, along with the characteristics noted above (Fig. 4.09).

Indeed, one of the springboards for this research was an early trawl of the internet, looking for durable and sustainable traditional housing types across the world that were also much loved and highly valued by owners, and occupants, and visitors. Some of the results of this search are pictured overleaf (Fig. 4.10). They share a quality which could be described as 'quietness'. They are unpretentious, simple, accessible and pleasant to look at. They make good street space: you can build a city out of them. And their creators are anonymous.

Notes to Chapter 4

1   Richard Jefferies, quoted in H E Huntley, The Divine Proportion, Dover Publications, 1970, p. 11.
2   Christopher Alexander, A Pattern Language, Oxford University Press, 1977, p. 115.
3   Dan Cruickshank, London: The Art of Georgian Building, Architectural Press, 1975, p. 39.
4   Richard Padovan, Proportion: Science, Philosophy, Architecture, Routledge, 1999.
5   Cruickshank, op. cit., p. 82.
6   Jan Gehl, Life Between Buildings: Using Public Space, Island Press, 2011, pp. 183–97.

Amsterdam   Berlin   Boston   Bruges   Copenhagen

Montevideo   New York   Oman   Osaka   Paris

Fig. 4.10: World housing archetypes, sharing a quality of quietness

Hanover   London   Marseilles   Menorca   Mexico City

Philadelphia   Quebec   San Francisco   Shanghai   St Johns   Tokyo

CHAPTER 5: SPACE AND LIGHT

Consider this image of a room (Fig. 5.01). It was painted by Henri Matisse in 1916 when he was living in a suburb of Paris at the height of the first world war. The painter gives us a very clear sense of the place. It could be a sitting room, or a bedroom, or even the corner of a kitchen. No matter. Simply called The Window, this painting describes a room in a city house, a room crossed with light, generous, filled with familiar useful objects, not ostentatious, simple yet elegant, a haven of safety from which to look out upon the world. There is privacy, but also a real connection with life outside. At the moment this image was created, the world was in great turmoil, but here there is optimism and a sense that a future of possibilities lies beyond. Sometimes a painting can capture an idea much better than a photograph, or a set of dimensions, or a performance standard.

Standards

Of course, the challenge in housing design is to create real environments of space and light using measurable and repeatable standards and dimensions, without losing the qualities that support us emotionally as well as practically.

In the UK, there is a tendency towards the exhaustive analysis of housing space standards that borders on a kind of reductio ad absurdum: a three-storey Parker Morris house in 1961 had a floor area of 100 square metres; a Housing & Communities Agency-sponsored house in 2010 had a floor area of 114 square metres.[1] Between the two, and very gradually increasing since the 60s, are seven other standards systems that have been applied. Are we to infer that the marginally increased standards applicable now are satisfactory? Anyone who measures up their own home for

Fig. 5.01: The Window, 1916 (oil on canvas), Henri Matisse, (1869 1954), Detroit Institute of Arts, US, City of Detroit Purchase © 2012 Succession H. Matisse/DACS, London. Photo: The Bridgeman Art Library

comparison will quickly understand that a single floor plate from a three-storey dwelling of 114 square metres (in total) will be cramped indeed.

It is not immediately obvious, but these are suggested minima rather than model standards, and they are often published with plan fragments to illustrate how it is possible to actually make a workable home within the prescribed and rather constricted dimensions (as for instance, the Space Standards Study diagrams in the new London Housing Design Guide[2]). This situation would be curious enough, but it is well known that housing in the private sector, not controlled by these recommendations, is regularly built to even smaller parameters. Indeed, according to research undertaken by CABE, the British build the pokiest homes in Europe, turning out the smallest new houses with the smallest average room sizes.[3] A contributory factor is the tendency in the UK to sell homes based on the number of rooms rather than on the overall usable floor area. This practice allows developers intent on maximising profit to reduce room size to the absolute workable minimum.

Room size/dwelling size

The average room size in the CABE study for all houses in Denmark was 29.4 square metres and the average for new dwellings there was 39.1 square metres. Compare this with the UK, where the average room size for all houses was 16.3 square metres and the average for new dwellings was (even less at) 15.8 square metres. Figures for average overall dwelling size are slightly more difficult to interpret because dwellings of all types and sizes are included in the average; but, again, the UK at 76 square metres for all new-build homes compares badly with Denmark at 137 square metres

(the largest in Europe), and the comparisons are even less flattering relative to Australian homes, which average 206 square metres, and US homes, which are the largest at 214 square metres. (Even the average Japanese home, at 92 square metres, is larger than the British one.) The figures for dwelling size and room size from our study tour were similarly divergent. It is as if we are talking about accommodating a different species in each country!

What size is the right size?

Deciding which modern standard is right may be difficult in the circumstances, but clearly the challenge of devising a modest, habitable room of optimum dimensions has been with us for millennia. In every society, there has been a stratum made up of people who are neither nobility nor serfs: in other words, people whose circumstances are those to which we all, in the modern world, now aspire. So when considering an ordinary person or family, and in the absence of extremes of wealth or poverty, what is optimum shape and size of a habitable room?

If we look at houses for ordinary citizens off a typical street in an ancient Greek city such as Kamiros in Rhodes, we note that the principal rooms generally measure about 4.5 metres across on the inside, and are very often square or near square in plan: a lesson from history. Square rooms of these dimensions can function well as living spaces, as kitchens and dining spaces, as double bedrooms or, if provided with two windows, can be subdivided to make two single-bed spaces (Figs 5.02, 5.03). This room width is generous without being extravagant, and the entire room can be provided with adequate daylight from windows on only one of the four sides (Fig. 5.08).[4]

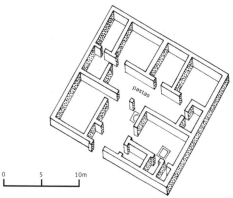

Fig 5.02: Citizens' houses in Kamiros, Rhodes, fifth century BC

Fig 5.03: Axonometric, a citizen's house, Olynthos Greece, fifth century BC

Perhaps not surprisingly, we notice that Le Corbusier, when conceiving his experimental workers' housing (realised as Quartiers Modernes Fruges at Pessac near Bordeaux in 1925), used cells of approximately 5 metres square (about 4.5 metres internally) to build up a range of four entirely different house types used across the site (Fig. 5.04).[5]

Cells of 4.5 metres square yield habitable rooms of about 20 square metres in area, or approximately the median figure between Danish and UK average standards (for all houses). In our prototype designs (Chapter 17) we have adopted this standard. Cells of this size aggregated to make a house on three storeys, sleeping five to six people, and yield a house of a minimum of 150 to 160 square metres, depending on the treatment of the entrance, circulation and storage spaces.

What height is the right height?

In our survey, and in wider discussions with others about housing design, high ceilings (of 2.7 to 4 metres) were universally appreciated and sought after. People described rooms with high ceilings as comfortable, generous and even dignified. Christopher Alexander links ceiling height with degrees of formality, from the very low/very intimate to the very high/very public.[6] Low ceilings demand intimacy, which may not always be appropriate, so higher ceilings provide greater flexibility. Alexander advocates varying ceiling height to suit the use pattern or cultural or climatic requirements of a particular situation, but this approach leads to a complex and expensive building cross section. High ceilings make all options possible.

In his excellent series for Channel 4,[7] Tom Dyckhoff interviewed neuroscientist Eve Edelstein at the Centre for Innovative Design Science, University of California. Wired up to record his emotional responses, he was taken into a virtual room, the ceiling of which was raised and lowered interactively. As the ceiling was raised, he said there was the sense of a weight lifting, and a more relaxed state was recorded on the monitoring equipment. Edelstein is

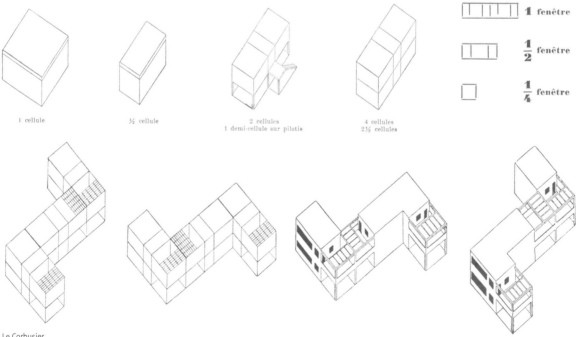

Fig. 5.04: Le Corbusier
La maison standardisée, 1924
Extrait de l'Œuvre Complète vol1, 1910-1929, p.69 © FLC: modular
system based on rectangles of approximately 4.5 metres square

compiling data that indicates a positive relationship between low ceilings and feelings of depression and stress.

Looking again at the example of Georgian houses, we note that ceiling heights of approximately 4 metres for the ground and first floors and 3 metres for higher floors were the norm, not only for so-called First Rate, but also for Second and Third Rate houses.[8] These rates (there were four in total) were enshrined in the Building Act of 1774, which set construction standards for houses built in London, including standards for room sizes and layouts.

The London Housing Design Guide provides guidance, and it links the appropriate height within a space to its depth, suggesting clear heights in a range from 2.6 to 3.2 metres. These figures are rather greater than the height commonly found in new-build housing of 2.3 metres. In our prototype we have adopted a floor-to-floor height of 3.15 metres, yielding ceiling heights typically varying from 2.6 to 2.8 metres depending on room function and the ceiling voids provided.

Light

In 2002, the Netherlands Research Institute for House, Urban and Mobility Studies undertook a review of building regulations in eight European countries in order to establish whether goals for this legislation were broadly similar in each country, as a first step towards further harmonisation of national standards.[9] This detailed study showed that there were fundamental differences in approach and content: notably, that England and Wales, alone among the eight countries, had no mandatory requirements in place for daylight standards and for ceiling heights. In order to provide guidance in the UK, however, there are recommended standards such as the requirements for daylight factors in the Code for Sustainable Homes, and the Daylight and Sunlight criteria in the London Housing Design Guide. These recognise obvious benefits to health and wellbeing derived from natural light, as well as acknowledging the energy credits associated with reducing dependence on artificial light and a contribution to passive energy gains in winter. There is a balance, however, to be achieved between the amount of daylight admitted and the associated heat losses in winter and heat gains in summer, both of which have to be mitigated. These are necessary technical assessments and trade-offs, but there also are other important qualitative judgements that need to be made.

Le Corbusier said, 'Space and light and order. Those are the things that men need just as much as they need bread or a place to sleep.'[10] His interest here was not in the quantity or the usefulness of space but in its aesthetic quality: that is, the beauty of space and of interconnecting volumes of space, revealed in light.

Corb and his generation were also standard bearers in architecture for the views of Auguste Rollier (1874–1954), a Swiss physician who pioneered the treatment of tuberculosis with sunlight. The view that sunlight was a balm for illness was widespread in Europe, and 'between the wars numerous beach resorts were built in southern Britain to draw people out of their bad housing, into healthy, life-enhancing sunshine. By 1933, sunlight was said to be a beneficial treatment for over 165 diseases.'[11]

Be that as it may, the fashionable interest at the time in light as a healer, and the new architectural freedoms made possible by concrete-and steel-frame construction, provided modern movement designers with both the enabling technology and the excuse to conceive space revealed in bright light as an object of aesthetic fascination. Free elevations and the use of large areas of glass were the means to this end. The window as a filter was lost.

The window

The window should modulate. It admits light, but it also creates a bridge between the inside and outside worlds. It is as important as

the threshold (Chapter 4). It has physical, practical and emotional implications.

These are partly exposed in an essay by Bruno Reichlin, 'The pros and cons of the horizontal window'.[12] The article records and analyses the arguments between supporters of the long narrow window (refined and perfected in the French tradition), and the horizontal format window, stretching across a room of unlimited width, made possible by 20th-century framed construction.

The vertical window 'allows the eye of the observer to wander downwards to the first and nearest spatial levels – street and garden – and horizontally to the middle and deeper levels – houses opposite, trees, hilly background – and upwards into the unlimited expanse of the sky'.[13] The horizontal window, on the other hand, 'condemns us to look at an eternal panorama'.[14]

The supporters of the horizontal format, however, were intrigued by the idea that it would 'tear open the protective shell of the private person' so that 'light pours in through this opening and de-mystifies the room and the objects; the sentimental objects regain their original solid, prosaic quality of practical tools'.[15]

Against the excitement of the modernists was the argument that 'inside there is this harsh, merciless light that destroys all feeling of calm and shelter',[16] and 'the scenery is there, in its direct immediacy, as if it were glued to the window because either a detached and calming effect is denied, or the transition from the nearby, familiar objects to the more distant ones is hidden from view, which significantly reduces the perception of three-dimensional depth'.[17] And more profoundly, 'the vertical window gives man a frame in line with his silhouette ... the vertical is the line of the upright human being, it is the line of life itself' (Fig. 5.06).[18]

In this treatise, vertical wins over horizontal. It should be read not as the expression of resistance to technical innovation, but as a plea that the nourishing qualities of the vertical window, the sense of inner seclusion combined with the possibility of

Fig. 5.06: Jean-Jacques Sempé: a window on the city

Antibes

Athens

Berlin

Brussels

Copenhagen

Havana

London

Melbourne

Mexico City

Montreal

New Orleans

New York

Nice

Paris

Fig. 5.07: Long windows, worldwide

engagement with the outside, should not be lost in the enthusiasm for experimentation. Auguste Perret, referring to supporters of the horizontal format, is quoted as saying that 'they are bewitched by volume; it is the only issue on their minds, and suffering from regrettable compulsion, they insist on devising combinations of lines without paying attention to the rest'.[19]

His concern, it seems, was in vain. Tall vertical windows, of refined proportions and sophisticated operation, were a feature of handsome 19th-century domestic buildings all over the world (Fig. 5.07). They were abandoned with the advent of the modern movement.

The point about windows – or, more generically, the parts of enclosure that admit light and allow views of the outside – is that they have complex significance, in both practical terms (control of light, ventilation, sound, heat gain and loss, security, privacy) and emotional terms (view of the weather and of the street, the glow of afternoon sun in the room, the charm of twilight). Where windows are treated merely as elements in the abstract composition of the facade, their meaning is impoverished.

The room

Looking again at the image of a quiet room by Matisse from the beginning of this chapter, we are obliged to try to identify why it works: something about the low sill of the window allowing a view of the street when one is sitting; something about the size of the room allowing easy and informal positioning of different pieces of furniture; something about the height of the room, implied by the long window; something about the warmth of the space created by daylight falling from the window right across the length of the floor, illuminating a bowl of flowers.

Fig. 5.08: A room of 4.5 metres square: a study, a bedroom, a living room: Vecindad, Mexico City

Notes to Chapter 5

1   Mapping Space Standards for the Home, CABE, 2010.
2   London Housing Design Guide, London Development Agency, 2010.
3   Improving the Quality of New Housing: Why the quality of our homes and neighbourhoods matters, Fig. 2: Comparison with European Union, CABE, 2010.
4   Lisa C. Nevett, House and Society in the Ancient Greek World, Cambridge University Press, 1999, p. 24.
5   Philippe Boudon, Pessac de Le Corbusier, Dunod, 1969, p. 32.
6   Christopher Alexander, A Pattern Language, Oxford University Press, p. 879.
7   Tom Dyckhoff, The Secret Life of Buildings, Channel 4, televised August 2011.

8   Dan Cruickshank, London: The Art of Georgian Building, Architectural Press, 1975, pp. 7–9.
9   Henk Visscher and Frits Meijer, Building Regulation for Housing Quality in Europe, Urban Planning Institute of the Republic of Slovenia, 2006.
10 Jacques Guitton (ed.), The Ideas of Le Corbusier, Braziller, 1981, p. 141.
11 Richard Cohen, Chasing the Sun, Simon & Shuster, 2010, p. 273.
12 Bruno Reichlin, 'The pros and cons of the horizontal window', Daidalos 13 (1984), 64–78.
13 ibid., p. 5.
14 ibid., p. 4, Reichlin quoting Auguste Perret.
15 ibid., p. 8, Reichlin quoting Le Corbusier.
16 ibid., p. 8, Reichlin quoting Baillie Scott.

17 ibid., p. 7, Reichlin quoting Dolf Sternberger.
18 ibid., p. 3, Reichlin quoting Marcel Zahar.
19 ibid., p. 1, Reichlin quoting Auguste Perret.

CHAPTER 6: CONSTRUCTION AND SUSTAINABILITY

Construction: volumetric, panellised, hybrid?

Expenditure on UK housing is currently estimated at about £42 bn (€51 bn) per annum (of which £28 bn (€34 bn) is privately funded and £14 bn (€17 bn) is publicly funded). This is a significant slice of the UK economy, and the objectives of the Government Construction Strategy (May 2011) rightly recognise the need for progressive reform in this sector, both in the procurement of buildings and in their design, fabrication and erection.[1]

Spending on housing is large, but should be larger.
Over the ten years to 2002, output of new homes was 12.5% lower than for the previous ten years. Despite a gradual increase from 2001 to 2007, the number of housing completions dropped dramatically in the face of the downturn since autumn 2007, with the annual completions in 2009 estimated below 150,000. At the same time, a significant rise in the number of households in the UK has been reported. DETR (2000) indicated a forecast increase by 3.8 million between 1996 and 2021 (based on 1996 statistics), equivalent to around 150, 000 each year. The Joseph Rowntree Land Enquiry (Barlow et al., 2002) suggested that around 225, 000 new homes will be needed each year in England alone to meet the demand arising from demographic changes and other needs up to 2016.[2]

The combined pressures of population increase and the need for construction efficiency are common to many world cities, and these are drivers towards so-called Modern Methods of Construction (MMC). At the core of these methods are advanced processes for house-building, including the off-site manufacture of building components and systems that are assembled or erected quickly on site. They are classified in the UK as follows:

Volumetric: three-dimensional units produced in a factory, fully fitted out before being transported to site, and stacked onto prepared foundations to form dwellings.

Panellised: flat panel units built in a factory and transported to site for assembly into a three-dimensional structure or to fit within an existing structure.

Hybrid: volumetric units integrated with panellised systems.

Sub-assemblies and components: larger components that can be incorporated into either conventionally built or MMC dwellings.

Non-off-site manufactured MMC: innovative methods of construction used on site, and the use of conventional components in an innovative way.[3]

The use of MMC promises a range of well-documented benefits including significant reductions in the cost of buildings and the time required to construct them, as well as significant improvements in quality both in the finished product and in the working conditions of construction operatives.

Nothing new?

There is a revolutionary ring to the rhetoric surrounding MMC, but prefabrication and off-site manufacture have been around for a long time. Indeed, the oldest standing town house in England,

Fig. 6.02: Traditional Tokyo house: a refined system grew out of local conditions

the Ancient High House in Stafford, is a building whose primary structure and cladding were entirely manufactured (in pieces of oak) away from the site and assembled rapidly in the High Street (Fig. 6.01). Tudor frame construction such as this was widely used where timber was in good supply but stonemasons were not.

Timber-frame construction which could be modularised, creating interior space of standardised dimensions, became a universal feature of traditional Japanese house-building.[4] In a country that has been regularly subjected to violent earthquakes, there was a need to devise a building form that could absorb movement, and that could be reconstituted quickly in the event of collapse (Fig. 6.02). The structurally independent timber-frame buildings that developed in these circumstances, dating from the 19th century and earlier, are now relatively scarce in cities like Tokyo, which has been ravaged not only by earthquakes but also by fires and by war (see Chapter 10). What is interesting, however, is that the culture of building individual houses on separate plots, using off-site prefabricated components and modules, has survived in Japan and continues to be the predominant approach.

Prefabrication in practice

Japan's leading house manufacturer, Sekisui Heim (see Chapter 10, Case study 2) (Fig. 6.03), is involved in what would be classified as 'volumetric' in the UK, and fabricates building blocks, complete with cladding on the outside and finished walls on the inside, that are simply aggregated together on site. This firm produces over 2,000 houses a year, in a vast mechanised factory staffed by over 1,000 employees. What is necessary to support a house-building industry dominated by volumetric prefabricators such as Sekisui Heim is a culture that regards the house as a disposable commodity – and such a culture has arisen from Japan's unique history. This phenomenon and this kind of demand are not present in other

Fig. 6.01: High House, Stafford: early prefabrication, built 1595

Fig. 6.03: Modern Japanese prefabricated house: Sekisui Heim, Tokyo

westernised cultures, so there is a question mark over the viability of an approach that is entirely volumetric outside Japan. One of the fundamental problems with this form of MMC is that it requires the creation of a large and sophisticated factory before a single unit can be created.

In Melbourne, the company Modscape, which operates from a large warehouse in a suburb of the city, undertakes another form of volumetric house-building, but one that appears to work better as a model for more typical western cultures (see Chapter 9, Case study 5) (Fig. 6.04). Here, the steel structural elements are bought in from independent manufacturers (to order) and merely assembled. All the cladding and fitting-out operations are executed under one roof, but each subcontract (electrical and plumbing work, partitioning, dry-walling, etc.) is completed by a different company. This commercial arrangement makes for greater flexibility and

Clockwise from above:

Fig. 6.04: An alternative system for prefabrication: Modscape, Melbourne

Fig. 6.05a and b: Forest Hills Gardens, New York: precast concrete housing under construction, 1918

Fig. 6.06: Forest Hills Gardens, New York: today

allows the company to tune its response to a fluctuating housing market in which volumetric house-building is a small component. This building system and the houses it produces are ideal for stand-alone situations, particularly where only a single storey is required. Modscape claims its designs would be technically suitable for city-centre locations; however, there is some doubt as to their appropriateness in terraced and medium-density communities.

In the search for situations where prefabricated housing has stood the test of time, and has been used to create viable and attractive communities that have lasted decades or longer, a pointer came from the book Home Delivery: Fabricating the Modern Dwelling.[5] This is an account of the history of off-site manufacture based on an exhibition at the Museum of Modern Art, New York, in 2008. It records an early initiative to create a city district of new homes at Forest Hills Gardens, Queens, New York, in 1918, using a precast concrete system that would be called 'panellised' in the UK (see Chapter 12, Case study 3) (Fig. 6.05).[6] This suburb is now extremely popular, and although the detailing of the houses imitates more conventional forms of construction the appearance of the buildings completely dispels the myth that concrete buildings will always look grey, brutal and severe (Fig 6.06).

Not far away is the now-famous Levittown, The US's first suburban housing development and the model for similar communities that came after it in all parts of the world (see Chapter 12, Case study 6 (Fig. 6.08). Here, the approach to standardised dwellings was akin to the now familiar flat-pack concept for furniture (Fig. 6.07). But like the Australian Modscape formula, this construction type is arguably unsuitable for dense cities.[7]

In London, the flat developments at Murray Grove in Islington and at Evelyn Road in the Royal Docks both employ a significant measure of prefabrication (see Chapter 11, Case studies 5 and 7) (Figs 6.09, 6.10). The former in particular uses steel box frames for the structure, in a similar way to the Modscape concept but

Above: Fig. 6.07: Levittown, New York: early 1950s' flatpack

Right: Fig. 6.08: Levittown, New York, today

clad with terracotta panels, to create a multistorey, multi-tenanted block. An obvious challenge for the use of such factory-assembled modules is the need to create the range of type, size and finish required by a conventional housing market.

Conclusions for construction

In summary, MMC as an approach is clearly needed in housing. To succeed, an appropriate form of MMC must be capable of creating a variety of attractive high-density housing configurations flexible internally and very robust externally; and an approach that does not require the investment of a large initial capital sum to create integrated factory-production facilities before the first dwelling can be delivered.

Fig. 6.09: Flats at Murray Grove, London

Fig. 6.10: Flats at Evelyn Road, London

SUSTAINABILITY: DRIVERS FOR CHANGE IN HOUSING

Stuart Hallett, Arup

Climate and CO_2 emissions

❝ In a time of increasingly high fuel prices, energy efficiency and the integration of renewable energy will become progressively more important in terms of both affordability and security. Many countries have become more import-reliant, and gradually more affected by the problems associated with fuel poverty. Geopolitical events continue to increase fuel prices, as well as drive volatility, and fuel prices globally are expected to increase by 60% by 2020. By 2050, it is anticipated that global temperatures will have continued to rise and greenhouse gas emissions are expected to have more than doubled if we carry on with 'business as usual'. To minimise future climate change, mitigation is a crucial goal; but adaptation will also be essential in numerous sectors, not least in building and housing. Designing for a future climate is important, as this will not only help to avoid fuel poverty but will also minimise the risk of homes overheating and alleviate flood risk. This means that future-proofing houses is essential, to meet both today's and tomorrow's needs.

Reducing energy use in homes has become a significant issue with the rise of climate-change concerns. CO_2 emissions arising from energy use account for more than 30bn tonnes each year (nearly half of which are the result of energy use in homes). This is an area of concern, given that the number of households is expected to grow by 67% globally by 2050. Homes in the UK account for approximately 27% of the total CO_2 emissions (Fig. 6.11).

Energy generation and supply

How to generate the energy to provide, among many other things, our household heating, hot-water, lighting, cooking and plug-in loads is also an increasingly important question. With overall energy use in the UK increasing by over 13% since 1970 and 11% since 1990, the obvious question is that of capacity of required energy.

The other key component of the question is that of sourcing the fuel and the means to generate that energy. With the recent historical reliance on imported gas, and locally sourced coal becoming an increasingly scarce and expensive commodity, other means of providing the energy are required. The strategies and policies underpinning this are still being resolved. However, there is an increasing move towards decentralised and on-site heat and power generation via renewables and high-efficiency low-carbon technologies.

The UK response

Research has concluded that the UK residential sector can deliver a 60% reduction in CO_2 emissions by 2050, in line with the targets outlined in the UK government's 2003 Energy White Paper. Such a reduction is essential in light of the growing impact of climate change. This represents a significant challenge, which requires some hard, but necessary, decisions if these savings are to be achieved.

Mechanisms have been put in place within the UK in an attempt to address the energy and CO_2 issues discussed above. These are predominantly financial incentives intended to rapidly grow the renewables and low-carbon energy-generation mix and promote energy efficiency in building design and operation, such as the Feed in Tariffs, Renewable Heat Incentive, the Carbon Reduction Commitment and, most recently, the Green Deal.

The overarching ambition is that all energy requirements of homes can be met in future decades by low-cost non-polluting sources. Research and development, and experience thus far, is showing this as a realistic, rather than impractical, possibility. However, over the next few years the rate of growth and diversification of the non-fossil-fuel energy technologies, and their contribution to the decarbonisation of each country's electricity grid, will be critical to success. Much can be learned from, and shared internationally, among those countries that have pioneered different technologies, to ensure that sound investment strategies are made by others. The contribution of wind and waste sources, which are both relatively new, are notable.

Benchmarks and standards

The minimum mandatory energy-and fuel-conservation standards for new housing within the UK are established through the Building Regulations Part L. These are the UK's interpretation and implementation of the EU Directive on the Energy Performance of Buildings.

Until recently the UK zero-carbon definition, to be introduced in 2016, was possibly the most stringent in the world, requiring all carbon emissions (including those from unregulated energy use such as cooking and plug-in appliances) to be addressed. However, in the March 2011 budget the UK government announced that zero carbon would be redefined to only require zero emissions from regulated energy use (ie the energy required to heat and cool a home and provide hot water and lighting). This is still a very challenging target for mainstream delivery, requiring considerable innovation over and above current practice and, typically, measures (Allowable Solutions) that reduce the emissions to levels that cannot normally be achieved by the design of the home. The new UK definition is now much closer to the requirements set out by the European Energy Performance of Buildings Directive.

Fig. 6.11: The first Level 6 UK home (Code for Sustainable Homes): Arup design engineers

A particular aspect of the minimum energy-and fuel-conservation standards is the Fabric Energy Efficiency metric. This is the measurement of the energy demand required for space heating and cooling, expressed in kWh of energy demand/m²/annum, and focuses on limiting the energy demands of heating and cooling the dwelling by passive measures only.

The UK remains a leader in the development of aspirational codes that have provided a stimulus for the design of homes to the most exacting sustainability standards. These homes, and in particular those built to Levels 4, 5 and 6 of the Code for Sustainable Homes (CfSH), provide valuable insight to inform the development of national standards in the UK and other countries.

Housing adaptation and mitigation

Adaptation addresses the impacts of unavoidable climate change. It is a response to impact risks that may directly affect human actions and the environment in which we live.

Adaptation is not associated with mitigation measures, which are ways of reducing greenhouse gas emissions by addressing the cause. However, climate-change mitigation and adaptation are complementary and both are vital in responding to climate change. While adaptation cannot change the weather, it can help to prevent some of its negative impacts and consequences. Climate change is likely to alter these risks in the future.

As our climate changes, the design and management of homes will need to consider how they can be changed to better cope with the new conditions. To plan a strategy based on historical climate data is no longer a sufficiently robust approach. It could lead to inadequate preparation, and, increasingly, government and insurers require climate changes to be factored in to decision-making. While it is not cost-free, planned adaptation is generally more cost-effective than last-minute reactive adaptation, which

may be too late in any event. In addition to providing residents with comfortable homes to live in, adaptation can deliver immediate local and national benefits.

Overheating

The predicted changes to the UK climate over the next few decades, in addition to the increasing envelope-performance standards, will require residential design to focus more on summertime comfort than has been the case in the past. With summers like that of 2003 becoming the norm rather than the exception, it will be more critical to our health and wellbeing that our dwellings provide us with an acceptable internal environment in very warm weather.

Many of these temperature-based and overheating-resultant adaptations can be passively addressed by relatively simple design decisions based upon building orientation, fenestration and envelope-material specification. Some of the considerations associated with building envelope materials are discussed below.

Thermal mass

There are conflicting views on the importance of thermal mass, solar gain and ventilation methods for sustainability in housing.

The influence of thermal mass on heating is shown to depend on the occupancy/gain scenario, insulation standard and climate. Insulation, climate, ventilation and orientation are shown to have the largest effects overall on heating energy requirements although thermal mass can also be important in specific climate and occupancy/gain cases.

It is shown that climate, thermal mass, shading, shuttering, ventilation and casual gains are all important factors in maintaining comfortable temperatures and avoiding summer overheating. High thermal mass, together with shading or shuttering, allows comfortable temperatures to be maintained without cooling (Fig. 6.12).

Overall, high-thermal-mass construction generally performs best

**STABILISING EFFECT OF THERMAL MASS ON
INTERNAL TEMPERATURE**

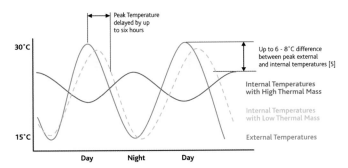

in houses built to the modern Building Regulations with their focus on highly insulated envelopes; the benefits are greatest in the southern UK climates. The exception is the case of very low occupancy/gains in the northern UK climates where low thermal mass may perform best.

Lightweight versus heavyweight construction

Research has illustrated the relatively poor performance, in terms of overall operational CO_2 emissions and passive regulation of internal temperatures, of thermally lightweight construction, as part of a response that includes solar, ventilation and internal heat gain control. It also shows the importance of how we operate our homes and the need to adapt this to climate change.

The issue of dealing with heatwaves is both a physical and a societal one. The tradition of buildings designed simply to maximise daylighting and passive solar heating for a cool, northern European climate will no longer be appropriate.

In contrast, traditional buildings in southern Europe have developed elements to minimise unnecessary heat gain and maximise passive cooling, through the use of shade, restriction of window areas, courtyards, shutters, and high thermal mass combined with hard surfaces to maximise heat exchange between internal air and building fabric.

For winter performance, the high thermal capacity works best with enhanced envelope thermal-insulation and airtightness standards, so reducing the overnight temperature drops and the resulting recovery periods for intermittent heating. This also enhances ability to absorb daytime heat gains and re-emit them during night-time periods of higher heat loss. As climate change reduces winter heating needs, it also prompts a review of the need for a full conventional central-heating system and increases the opportunities for 'zero heating' homes.

In summary, mitigation of climate-change effects can be achieved by designing homes with thermally massive passive features. This enables us to adapt the way we operate our homes to offset the expected temperature increases. On the other hand, thermally lightweight homes would result in substantially higher room temperatures and levels of discomfort.

Conclusions for sustainability

There is a variety and a wide range of requirements that a dwelling in a modern urban environment needs to respond to and can aspire to. The overarching questions of sustainability, what this means and how it is achieved can be answered in a number of different ways.

The above describes some of the drivers of sustainability, the UK response and some of the methodologies employed to answer the big questions and deliver tangible results. **"**

Notes to Chapter 6

1   Government Construction Strategy, The Cabinet Office, May 2011.
2   Chris Goodier and Wei Pan, The Future of UK Housebuilding, December 2010, RICS Research.
3   Modern Methods of Construction: BeAware Sector Report, March 2009, BRE File Library.
4   Norbert Schoenauer, 6,000 Years of Housing, W.W Norton & Company, 2000, pp. 204–8.
5   Barry Bergdoll and Peter Christensen, Home Delivery: Fabricating the Modern Dwelling, 2008, Museum of Modern Art, New York.
6   ibid., p. 16.
7   http://tigger.uic.edu/~pbhales/Levittown/building.html

Fig. 6.12: Graph: effects of thermal mass. Source: The Concrete Centre

CHAPTER 7: COST AND VALUE

Earlier chapters have made the case, in qualitative terms, for low-rise high-density urban housing that is flexible, adaptable, energy efficient and capable of being repeated and scaled to form coherent and successful communities. Let us use the expression 'city houses' to describe this form.

There are parts of the core areas of most modern cities where land values are so high that residential plot ratios of 3:1 or greater are needed before development appraisals become viable. In these zones, city houses will not generate sufficient value to justify land cost. In rural and outlying suburban areas, on the other hand, where the land-cost ingredient in the equation and the sales values are relatively low, it will be the build cost that determines whether or not a scheme is viable , and it is likely that relatively high-density and relatively sophisticated housing products will be too expensive here (putting aside, for the moment, local planning policy issues). So the fertile ground for city houses lies in the area peripheral to the central business district, where land values are high enough to support good-quality product but not so high that they require very tall buildings with extremely high densities.

This phenomenon is found in many world cities, and it is a bit like the concept of the Goldilocks Zone.[1] In the story 'Goldilocks and the Three Bears', a little girl selects from sets of three choices, avoiding extremes of size and temperature. The concept is used to describe the planetary zone between the sun and deep space that may be favourable to life, or alternatively the galactic habitable zone, measured from the centre of a galaxy. The Goldilocks Zone for city houses requires a balance of cost and value that must be 'just right', or at least within an acceptable band. However, the ability of developers to perceive that the right value can be achieved, and the ability of constructors to create this value at the right cost in a particular zone, determines whether city houses will grow there. What follows are contributions from two distinguished individuals from the property industry. They are looking at this particular challenge from different perspectives, but they are both concerned with helping to define and expand the zone in which city houses can thrive.

NEW DRIVERS FOR COST AND QUALITY IN HOUSING
Ben de Waal, Residential, Davis Langdon (an AECOM company)

❝ There is obviously a significant range of building designs that covers a multitude of quality and cost options (Fig. 7.01). The challenge, as ever, is to optimise the cost/value relationship so that every pound spent increases value by more than a pound. The correlation is not always clear because value is more often seen as a derivative of market demand and the ability to pay rather than of the quality and cost of the underlying asset. This drives a mentality of cost reduction to increase margin rather than a mentality of value maximisation through enhancement of the product or the environment.

Unfortunately, given sensitivities over working capital and sales risk, the default position is too often to pursue a lower-value lower-cost option. The objective must be to get higher quality without also increasing cost, and this suggests that the industry should take more of a manufacturer's approach to house-building, but success in doing so to date has been mixed.

The impetus for such an approach is driven by several other needs:

First, improvement in the environmental performance and design quality of new homes remains one of the cornerstones of the government's housing strategy. This necessarily shifts the focus to Modern Methods of Construction (MMC) or modular/volumetric forms of construction. A tightening of quality and environmental standards is likely to tip the balance in favour of manufactured

Notes:

1)
All figures are based upon a location factor of south-east UK, excluding Greater London
2)
All residential figures assume CfSH Level 4 (subject to sustainability strategy)
3)
All figures exclude infrastructure and external works costs
4)
The apartment rate assumes a net-to-gross efficiency of 80%
5)
The above figures include main contractor on-costs and preliminaries

Residential Sector: High Level Costs @ 2nd Quarter 2012 (source Davis Langdon)

Fig. 7.01: Housing cost comparison

solutions, especially when labour costs start to rise.

Second, improvement in the speed of construction, so that assets can become income-producing or be sold sooner, thereby reducing the pressure on working capital, is very desirable.

Third, embracing a manufacturing approach to house-building yields dramatic improvements in the energy efficiency and waste reduction associated with construction, as well as significant improvements in the working conditions of operatives (Fig 7.02).

Fourth, the emergence of better-informed and more demanding buyers, who take as much interest in the running cost of their homes as they do in the miles-per-gallon performance of their car, requires a clear response from the industry.

In our drive to move forward, we are competing against some very real constraints:

There is inertia in moving away from the tried-and-tested traditional forms of construction. The supply chains are established, and the costs and risks associated with these tried-and-tested forms are fully understood.

The default approach to appraisals focuses too much on cost reduction rather than on value creation. In most development appraisals the land cost is the residual element, so the emphasis necessarily focuses on sales value forecasts, finance costs and product cost as the main variables to manage. However, we are operating in an increasingly risk-averse environment, and public and private sector developers alike are far more inclined to pursue increased margins through cost reductions that are easier to control and predict than through product enhancements aimed at delivering higher sales values that are ultimately outside their control and more difficult to predict.

There is an unstable and unpredictable demand for non-traditional forms of construction. Hence, we have seen a lack of investment in R&D and capital investment in production plants that could really shift the emphasis to manufactured forms. Research and Development tax credits help, but do not go far enough. There also needs to be an incentive for the developer to buy the necessary R&D, such as tax credits or capital allowances on manufactured components. Indeed, government policy and the Housing and Communities Agency support could play a major role in the development of MMC, for it relies on volume guarantees to support research and the capital investment needed for it to compete on cost terms with traditional alternatives.

The Government Construction Strategy (2011) reminded us of the importance of an efficient construction industry to the success of the UK economy.[2] New approaches to procurement aimed at reducing construction costs by 20% sit at the heart of that strategy and challenge the industry to develop more integrated teams, with designers, other professional consultants and constructors offering an integrated proposition and key manufacturers involved in developing the design.

The ambition must be achieved without falling foul of the same negative 'prefab' connotations witnessed in the 1960s. The danger is that the industry goes forward with solutions that are either wholly traditional or wholly 'modern' (a manufacturer's approach: MMC). But the answer probably lies in a combination of both (see also Chapter 6).

Perhaps the optimum solution is one that combines the modern and traditional forms of construction. The former could deliver the main structure and envelope through the use of standardised or cellular forms (that still yield aesthetic variety). The latter could deliver the substructure, fit out and services elements that need to remain flexible to accommodate variable ground conditions for a particular site, as well as addressing changes in technology and consumer taste that influence interior design. The two could and should coexist happily. **"**

Fig. 7.02: New town house, Hammersmith, London: embracing modern methods of construction, the prototype, Chapter 17

**REALISING THE WHOLE WORTH OF SUSTAINABLE
DEVELOPMENT: THE TRUE COST AND VALUE OF CITY HOUSES**
Yolande Barnes, Head of Residential Research, Savills

" Standard methods of valuation and appraisal may show that
urban streetscapes are less profitable than typical 'greenfield'
suburban houses. But developers who use these methods
could miss out on doubling their annual profits.

This statement may appear inherently contradictory, but the
construction of good city housing is daily impaired by the way that
the property industry operates in the UK, and elsewhere. The best
way of demonstrating this is to illustrate how the additional costs of
building high-quality city houses might be viewed in two ways and
how a square-foot appraisal hides real-world, whole-place value.
This 'whole-place value' is both tangible – in the immediate term
and over the longer term – and intangible – being realised in social
and environmental value. This section shows how different methods
and approaches to the issue of city-making can significantly affect
development outcomes.

Put simplistically, if a house builder, having bought a site,
does a conventional comparison of build costs per square foot
against achievable market value in a location, they are liable to find
themselves looking at significantly higher costs and lower profits for
a city house than for a conventional, suburban unit (Fig 7.03).

Such a simple appraisal would, and does, put house builders
off even considering starting down the route of building city
houses (unless the planning system insists on it). But the focus by
conventional house builders on the per-square-foot building costs
and capital values threatens to cheat the development industry of
additional profit. More importantly, it deprives the country of great new
neighbourhoods that a wide variety of people would want to live in.

New, high-quality urban landscapes are few and far between.
Where they do exist, the real estate created has a demonstrably
higher value than suburban or 'flatted' housing would have on the
same site. Increasing evidence has mounted that there is additional,
hidden, value in city building that is not captured in the above
equation:

First, the value of a city house, if it is done well, can be much
higher than the equivalent standard developer's unit.

Second, where established historical high-density models for
low-rise buildings are used, more square feet can be built on the
same plot of land.

Third, markets can be broadened and diversified by building a
variety of unit types (there is a particular shortage of desirable family
units in many urban locations, for example), and this can mean
higher rates of sale and enhanced values as well as sale receipts.

Fourth, additional value and revenues can be derived from the
use of some buildings for commercial and mixed uses.

There is also evidence that capital appreciation over time
is better for sustainable urban development than for standard
suburban housing types. This should make good high-intensity city
development more attractive to a variety of longer-term investors,
and enhance the investment value to potential landlords.

The real mystery is why, in a world where capital is very actively
seeking added value from all manner of asset classes, there is not
more high-quality high-intensity mixed-use flexible urban property
being built.

Turning the above appraisal into a whole-site appraisal and incorporating evidence of value uplift from various Savill's research projects can tell a very different story (Fig 7.04).

Looking at this equation, the question changes from 'Why build streets of city houses?' to 'Why build anything else?' Answering this question requires us to understand more about developers' business models, their history and how they may change in future.

Housing development in the 20th century became almost entirely suburban in context throughout the western world as the automobile became a dominant force and the development of roads and urban streets gave way to bypasses and trunk roads. Semi-detached and detached houses built on agricultural land at low densities with gardens of their own became the aspiration of the masses. Town and country planning and its allocation of land followed this paradigm for much of the second half of the century.

The private house-building industry catered to this demand, evolved and adapted solely to fulfil these aspirations – and did so very well over many decades. Most importantly, the methods of financing and appraising cost, risk and returns evolved alongside the house-building industry, whose principal aim was maximising return on capital employed at minimal risk. The business methods of the industry revolved around generating a return on capital employed to shareholders on an annual basis. This meant, and continues to mean, that capital outlay is minimised, especially at the outset of the development process. The use of options to purchase land at low near-agricultural values was an important element of minimising capital outlay, as was cheap debt to enable development gearing. This means that the value added to land by the developer has long been shared with financiers and landowners.

While this business model worked well for much of the 20th century, two things now threaten to render it obsolete. The first is the disappearance of cheap, easily available debt funding. The second is 'urban renaissance' and the increasing restriction on the supply of easily developable, greenfield sites.

The approach of the millennium saw a new spate of urbanisation, which began to reverse the dominant trend of the 20th century for people to leave the cities for the suburbs. This renewed demand for urban living has combined with a need to revitalise and regenerate old urban centres in industrial decline. But the old methods of urban development had been lost with Nash and Cubitt and their ilk (Fig 7.05). The urban landowner landlords, the leasehold system and widespread private renting, which had

Single Dwelling: £ per square foot (×10 £ per square metre)	Suburban housing model	City housing model
Land cost, say	100	100
Build cost	100	150
Sales value (based only on existing, local, achieved prices)	300	300
Developer surplus	100	50

Fig 7.03: Simple single-dwelling appraisal

Whole site: £	Suburban housing model	City housing model
Land cost, say	5,000,000	5,000,000
Build cost	5,000,000	15,000,000
Sales value (based on observed sustainable urbanism premium, higher density and additional receipts for other uses)	15,000,000	33,000,000
Developer surplus	5,000,000	13,000,000

Fig 7.04: Whole-site development appraisal

Fig. 7.05: Thomas Cubitt houses, Pimlico, London: lessons from the past

been so much a part of the business models that built Britain's major cities before the end of the 19th century, had been lost in the 20th. The business models to build great streets of city houses were missing.

Complex and capital-intensive land-preparation processes and long build periods, together with new marketing strategies, were not the forte of the suburban house builders. Little surprise, then, that the first pioneers of residential urban regeneration were innovative newcomers, helped, it has to be said, by an era of the easiest debt finance we will probably ever know and a wide choice of cheap land and disused buildings in or very near city centres.

These pioneering urbanists borrowed some of their business models from the commercial property world. They did not build streets, they built blocks. Flatted developments rather than terraces were the norm. The more capital-intensive build and high-risk processes of urban master-planning and infrastructure installation were counterbalanced by high return on capital, resulting from (initially) cheap land and even cheaper finance and then increasing house-price inflation. The ability of developers to sell apartments off plan, in advance of completion, to a rising number of private landlords was also of importance in the new world of urban residential development.

Since the dramatic change in the financial and business environment, rendered after 2007, many of these methods of urban development are no longer available to protagonists. Low levels of capitalisation in the house-building industry mean that realising the enhanced value of city housing over suburban housing is simply not an option to many developers who just do not have the sums available to do so. This means that despite demonstrable demand from families and renters for city properties, it remains difficult to deliver them using conventional methods.

Time, then, for new entrants: long-term investors able to develop and hold new pieces of city over a long period of time and interested in the long-term income and value that it generates. The world is full of such equity-seeking income streams. It is up to the property industry to first understand and then make the case for sustainable urbanism. We need to start by re-evaluating the methods of development appraisal that our industry uses. Consider this chapter a call to do so. **"**

Notes to Chapter 7

1   http://science.nasa.gov/science-news/science-at-nasa/2003/02oct_goldilocks

2   Government Construction Strategy, The Cabinet Office, May 2011.

PART 2: CITIES

Introduction to Part 2

This part of the book contains case studies from nine world cities (Copenhagen, Melbourne, Tokyo, London, New York, Paris, Berlin, Mexico City and Shanghai). We have critically reviewed all the case studies using the parameters identified in Part 1, so that the accounts of each home are not just descriptive but provide assessments in a consistent format that relates to the analysis presented earlier. This approach makes it easier to draw comparisons and form conclusions. There is a chapter for each city, each with the same format.

There is a one-page summary of the historical and physical contexts in which the various forms of housing in the city are found. This is accompanied by a set of statistics on population, density, growth and other comparative measures including the unit cost of public transport, average earnings and the average cost of a dwelling.

There is an aerial view of the central area of the city, indicating the location of each case study property, with an inset view of the entire conurbation showing the boundary used for the calculation of population and density as a colour tone.

There are two larger case studies for which we undertook in-depth interviews with the residents. These studies give values for the density, plot ratio, cost, floor area and age of the property. The statistics are followed by a description of the features of the home, using headings from Part 1 of the book (Chapters 2 to 7), to give a degree of parallelism in the accounts for each larger study and to enable meaningful comparisons to be made. An aerial photo of the plot with its context is provided, together with photographs of the inside and outside of the residence, and scaled plans. We felt it was important to undertake an evaluation of each home, explicitly based on our criteria, so that the case studies were not merely descriptive and so that in some way the performance of the properties could be compared. The evaluation is presented in each case as a marking out of 100.

Following the larger case studies, in each city chapter there are four to six smaller studies. For each example we have provided images and background information and have made an evaluation in the same form as that used for the larger studies.

The QR icon here (www.thenbs.com/a-house-in-the-city) provides online access to further images and full scoring data. The book gives only the totals under each parameter heading, but readers may find it interesting to look at the full scorings, which provide evaluations for every question.

Units for statistics

City population density

Figures for population size and density relate to the area outlined in colour tone on the inset aerial plans. For each city, this zone typically includes the central business district and the inner residential areas (or inner suburbs), but excludes the outer suburbs. The population density calculated for this zone has been provided to give a comparative context for the plot-density figures for the case-study properties, most of which fall within the inner city zone.

Plot density

This is expressed in habitable rooms per hectare (HR/ha). Habitable rooms include bedrooms, living rooms, studies, dining rooms and larger kitchens, but exclude bathrooms and very small enclosed kitchens. In addition to the dwelling footprint, the plot area includes a portion of the access road of the same width as the plot, extending from the plot boundary to the centre of the road. For higher multistorey developments which sit in areas of open space that are part of the scheme, a portion of that open space (generally defined by the midpoint between tall buildings) has been included in the plot area.

Plot ratio

This is expressed as the ratio of gross internal floor area (the total area inside the enclosing walls of the home) to net site area (measured to the edge of the plot).

How the homes were assessed

We considered whether to use an established set of criteria to evaluate our examples, and looked in particular at the set devised by CABE, in the National Standard for Homes and Neighbourhoods, called Building for Life. These constitute their 'vision of functional, attractive, and sustainable housing', and on the face of it they sounded as if they would cover very similar ground to the criteria we had identified. However, it became clear that more than half of the CABE criteria were concerned with the larger community, and with other, broader planning issues such as parking and the integration of cars and pedestrians. Because our focus has been principally on the individual home and its immediate surroundings, we decided to stick with the criteria we had identified (in Chapters 2 to 7). However, we have used the question-based assessment structure devised by CABE.

Each of the questions below is given a mark out of four. This yields a total assessment score out of 100.

Density and Urban Form

Is the model repeatable and scale-able?	4
Does it reach a desirable density (of 450 HR/ha or more)?	4
Does it allow the creation of good streets and urban space? Can you make a city out of it?	4
Does it avoid the creation of anonymous open space and semi-public access space?	4
Does it allow easy and close visual contact with activities on the ground and in the street?	4
	20

Flexibility and Adaptability

Is there an absence of hierarchy in the main rooms?	4
Is there an absence of loadbearing internal walls?	4
Is it easy to add to, update and/or change the services?	4
Is the circulation permeable?	4
Is it possible to extend the structure?	4
	20

Appearance and Threshold

Is the design authentic?	4
Does it have good scale?	4
Does it have good proportions?	4
Does it display economy of means?	4
Does the treatment of the threshold provide a good transition with an appropriate level of detachment?	4
	20

Space and Light

Are the principal habitable rooms big enough (about 20 square metres in area)?	4
Are the ceilings high (at least 2.6 metres)?	4
Do the windows allow a view of the outside and the street when a person is sitting? Can they be opened?	4
Is the quantity of light sufficient (glazing equal to about 20% of the floor area), without being overpowering?	4
Is there access to some private open space (of about 5 square metres per person)?	4
	20

Construction and Sustainability

Does the construction use sustainable materials that are local to the site and/or to the point of manufacture?	4
Does the construction employ any off-site manufacturing techniques?	4
Can the primary structure and cladding elements be erected rapidly on site, and ideally without scaffolding?	4
Does the construction perform well in terms of energy consumption, airtightness and heat recovery?	4
Does the design include measures to harvest rainwater and/or generate thermal energy or electricity?	4
	20

100

Tokyo Copenhagen

Melbourne London

New York Berlin

Mexico City Paris Shanghai

CHAPTER 8

COPENHAGEN

CITY STATISTICS

GREATER COPENHAGEN REGION POPULATION	1,213 800
AVERAGE GROSS DENSITY, PEOPLE PER KM² (PER HA)	6,200/KM² (62/HA)
POPULATION GROWTH RATE PER ANNUM	2%
COST OF METRO TICKET FOR ONE STOP, € (LOCAL)	€3.20 (24DKK)
AVERAGE EARNINGS PER ANNUM, € (LOCAL)	€48,600 (362,600 DKK)
AVERAGE HOUSE PRICE TO AVERAGE INCOME RATIO	7:1
AVERAGE NUMBER OF CARS PER 1,000 PEOPLE	260

Copenhagen has a human scale; its calm architectural style reflects the Danes' unique design sensitivity and it consistently achieves top ratings in international lifestyle magazines. Its public transport and cycle infrastructures are exemplary: Its metro runs 24 hours and with over 390 kilometres of designated bike lanes, approximately 40 % of its inhabitants commute by bike on a daily basis.

Copenhagen was founded within a fortress built by Bishop Absalon in 1160 and, with its excellent harbour, grew rapidly. It has been Denmark's capital since 1417. Following the second world war, many Copenhagen neighbourhoods had deteriorated into slums. In 1947, an ambitious urban renewal policy, 'the Finger Plan' (Fingerplanen), redeveloped much of the city and divided the Copenhagen metropolitan area into five suburban areas. The S-train lines follow the Finger Plan, and green wedges and highways are built between the fingers.

The city intends to be the world's first carbon neutral metropolis by 2025, introducing policies that increase environmental awareness and improve construction sustainability. As part of this strategy, Copenhagen requires green roofs for all new buildings with roof slopes of less than 30 degrees. By 2015, all residents should be able to reach a park or beach on foot in less than 15 minutes.

Housing Typologies

The architecture in Copenhagen is beautiful and diverse: 18th-century pastel-coloured canal houses are found in the centre; high-density megablocks in the outlying districts and modest terraced housing schemes are interspersed in the central area with sharply designed apartment blocks.

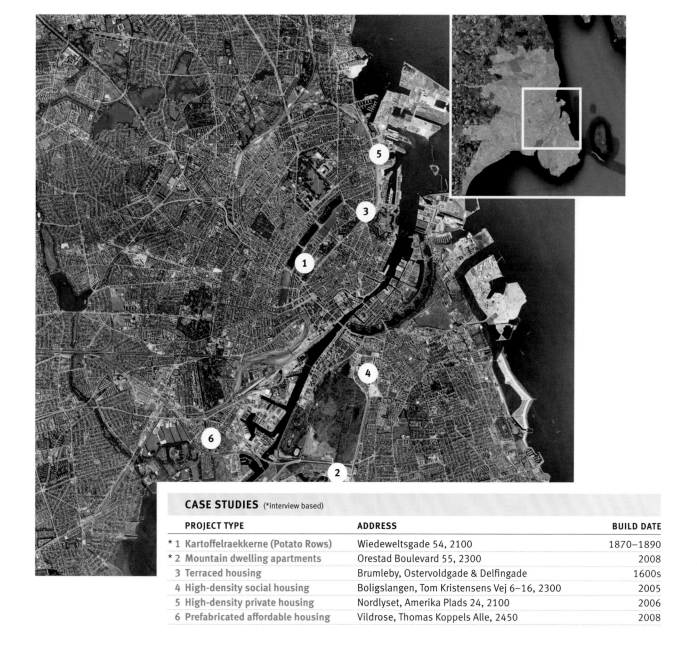

CASE STUDIES (*interview based)

PROJECT TYPE	ADDRESS	BUILD DATE
* 1 Kartoffelraekkerne (Potato Rows)	Wiedeweltsgade 54, 2100	1870–1890
* 2 Mountain dwelling apartments	Orestad Boulevard 55, 2300	2008
3 Terraced housing	Brumleby, Ostervoldgade & Delfingade	1600s
4 High-density social housing	Boligslangen, Tom Kristensens Vej 6–16, 2300	2005
5 High-density private housing	Nordlyset, Amerika Plads 24, 2100	2006
6 Prefabricated affordable housing	Vildrose, Thomas Koppels Alle, 2450	2008

1 Kartoffelraekkerne (Potato Rows)

Resident: Svend Larsen
Wiedeweltsgade 54, 2100

The Potato Row houses – low-cost high-quality terraced homes designed to alleviate the poor living conditions for working-class families – are now Copenhagen's most sought-after homes. Svend Larsen has lived here with his family for 20 years.

Density and urban form
Potato Row houses strike the right balance between urban form, convivial street life and residential privacy, achieving good urban intensity at four storeys (including basement). Residents and community are prioritised over cars within the narrow lanes; trees, picnic tables and play structures act as traffic-calming features as well as enhancing the vibrancy of the street life.

Flexibility and adaptability
The robust external and brick party walls enable the 'soft' timber interior to be torn down and reconfigured, accommodating a range of living patterns over time; the internal staircase position permits the house to be divided into apartments.

Appearance and threshold
The houses along the Potato Rows follow a simple symmetry and proportion in window layout and brick treatment that binds the overall character of the street. Small front yards blur the transition from private to public space and the lack of kerbs allows residents to consider the street as their domain. People often sit out in the street, watching their children play, and each individual terrace has its own sense of community and identity.

Dwelling Plans

Key:

A Front patio
B Living
C Dining
D Kitchen
E Rear courtyard
F Bedroom
G Balcony
H Office
I   Living

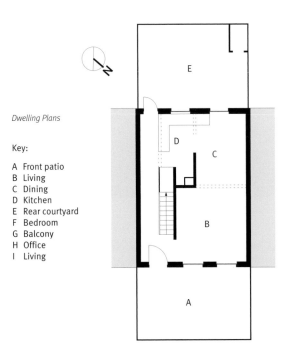

Ground Floor

First Floor

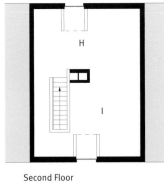

Second Floor

0m 1 2 3 4 5

Space and light

The houses are planned in rows, with small back yards and with windows in front and back elevations. In addition, each dwelling has generous ceiling heights and clear spans. The communal street has been appropriated as a much-valued outdoor extension to the homes.

Construction and sustainability

The houses were constructed with locally sourced materials and planned as simple terraces to save costs. This form of terraced house is an economic and sustainable form of construction whose open structure affords great flexibility and thereby longevity. Dual-aspect windows provide cross ventilation.

Cost and value

These low-cost houses were constructed by building societies in the 1890s, and today are regarded as prime real estate and exemplars of urban residential planning ●

CASE STUDY DATA

Density (HR/ha):	500
Plot ratio:	1.5:1
Cost to buy:	€5,375/m² (40,667 DKK/m²)
Buy cost as a multiple of average earnings:	x 15.25
Floor area:	150m²
Plot area:	100m²
Outdoor private amenity space:	Rear yard 25m² and front garden 23m²
Floor-to-ceiling height:	2.5m
Floor area per habitable room:	13m²
Age of building (and style):	1870–90, terraced house
Preferred room in the house:	Loft room

Above left: Svend Larson and his wife

Above centre: The front elevation is composed using simple proportions and symmetry

Above right top: The communal street is treated as an extension to the homes

Above right lower: The ground-floor living and dining room

SCORES

DENSITY & URBAN FORM	20
FLEXIBILITY & ADAPTABILITY	18
APPEARANCE & THRESHOLD	19
SPACE & LIGHT	17
CONSTRUCTION & SUSTAINABILITY	7
TOTAL	81

2 **Mountain Dwelling Apartments**

Residents: Jane and Thomas
Orestad Boulevard 55, 2300

Designed by Danish architects Bjarke Ingels Group (BIG), the 80 apartments above a six-storey car park are intended to 'combine the splendours of the suburban backyard with the social intensity of urban density'. The courtyard apartments scale the diagonally sloping roof of the car park from street level, creating an artificial south-facing 'mountainside'.

Jane and Thomas, a young professional couple, are among the first to own a flat in this development.

Density and urban form

Only one third of the 30,000-square-metre scheme is built for housing; the remainder is used for parking. All apartments are detached from the surrounding streets and there are no shops or amenities at ground level. The private 'back yard' of each flat opens up as a terrace, part of the 'mountainside', and contributes to a sense of community. The complex is stunning yet idiosyncratic in form, and could not be incorporated into an urban grain.

Above: Private terrace space

Opposite page:

Above: Private gardens open up to a semi-private green corridor

Centre: Flexible living spaces

Below: Mountain Dwellings, disconnected from street level

Dwelling Plan

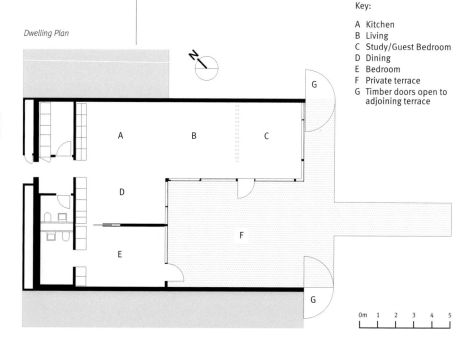

Key:

A Kitchen
B Living
C Study/Guest Bedroom
D Dining
E Bedroom
F Private terrace
G Timber doors open to adjoining terrace

0m 1 2 3 4 5

Flexibility and adaptability
The apartments are standardised with clear-span open layouts, and sliding doors enable the spaces to combine and separate as needed. The spare room doubles as a study or guest bedroom.

Appearance and threshold
This bold and visually arresting scheme mimics nature in its architectural form. Entry to the apartments is via a sloping elevator that climbs through the brightly coloured car park levels and cavernous enclosed space.

Space and light
The private terrace and garden occupies almost as much space as the interior and is cherished even during winter. The full-height glazed facade opens the interior living areas to the outdoors, and natural daylight, high ceilings and an open living layout increase the sense of space in the relatively large apartment.

Construction and sustainability
The structure of the car park is steel frame and the 'mountainside' terraces are made of in-situ concrete in a repetitive pattern. The apartment facades are timber clad, and terraces incorporate rainwater harvesting which feeds an automatic watering system for private green roofs. All dwellings face south and turn their backs on the main access road.

Cost and value
Despite the property being perfect for their current lifestyle, Jane and Thomas wish to move on to 'our own space, on the ground: a space that is completely ours'. The car park is usually empty as the monthly rental of 540 DKK (73 euros) is unaffordable ●

SCORES

DENSITY & URBAN FORM	3
FLEXIBILITY & ADAPTABILITY	9
APPEARANCE & THRESHOLD	12
SPACE & LIGHT	16
CONSTRUCTION & SUSTAINABILITY	9
TOTAL	49

CASE STUDY DATA

Density (HR/ha):	357
Plot ratio:	1.19:1
Cost to buy:	€3,575/m² (26,606 DKK/m²)
Buy cost as a multiple of average earnings:	x 7.25
Floor area:	109m²
Plot area:	33,000m²
Outdoor private amenity space:	102m², of which 40m² is usable garden area
Floor-to-ceiling height:	2.5m
Floor area per habitable room:	26m²
Age of building (and style):	2008, contemporary terraced apartments
Preferred room in the house:	Garden and kitchen

Small front gardens and level thresholds in Brumleby's secondary lanes

3 Terraced Housing
Brumleby and various sites including
Ostervoldgade & Delfingade 1600s

Two to three storeys in height, these
houses were economically built in the
1600s and later. Their mid-city density is
typical for inner suburbs of Copenhagen.
Brumleby is the earliest example of social
terraced housing. Its central secondary
lanes – big enough for cars to drive
through, but private enough to create a
semi-public space – are effectively used as
gardens and children's play spaces.

SCORES	
DENSITY & URBAN FORM	19
FLEXIBILITY & ADAPTABILITY	13
APPEARANCE & THRESHOLD	19
SPACE & LIGHT	14
CONSTRUCTION & SUSTAINABILITY	6
TOTAL	71

4 High-density Social Housing
Boligslangen, Tom Kristensens Vej 6–16,
2300 2005

Boligslangen (Serpentine House), designed
by Domus Arkitekter, is situated on a
former industrial site. The high-density
linear block, with 320 dwellings of varied
sizes, weaves a continuous line through
expansive lawns and canals. The outlook
from the flats is pleasant, and full-height
glazing gives good spatial and light quality,
but the architecture is anonymous, brutal
and detached.

SCORES	
DENSITY & URBAN FORM	6
FLEXIBILITY & ADAPTABILITY	6
APPEARANCE & THRESHOLD	5
SPACE & LIGHT	12
CONSTRUCTION & SUSTAINABILITY	2
TOTAL	31

Above: Set within expansive green space
Left: High-rise living

Weak connection with the public square adjacent

5 High-density Private Housing
Nordlyset, Amerika Plads 24, 2100 2006

Nordlyset is a six-storey, white-polished block in the new densely built-up block district of Amerika Plads, containing 102 flats ranging in size from 70 to 150 square metres. The apartments possess two balconies, front and back, that are carved into the facade, with protruding glass panels in pale colours. Shops and a cafe are located on the ground floor and the courtyard forms a roof over the underground car park.

SCORES	
DENSITY & URBAN FORM	11
FLEXIBILITY & ADAPTABILITY	9
APPEARANCE & THRESHOLD	14
SPACE & LIGHT	19
CONSTRUCTION & SUSTAINABILITY	4
TOTAL	57

6 Prefabricated Affordable Housing
Vildrose, Thomas Koppels Alle, 2450 2008

The scheme is composed of 38 shared-ownership houses at 85 square metres each, designed to accommodate a family of four. It contributes to Copenhagen's ambition to build 5,000 affordable housing units. The prefabricated design was inspired by contemporary and traditional Danish architecture. Flexibility, natural light and daylight through skylights were important design factors. The houses share a large lawn, which is intensively used as communal space.

SCORES	
DENSITY & URBAN FORM	17
FLEXIBILITY & ADAPTABILITY	13
APPEARANCE & THRESHOLD	20
SPACE & LIGHT	17
CONSTRUCTION & SUSTAINABILITY	17
TOTAL	84

Small front yards are ideal for community activities

CHAPTER 9

MELBOURNE

CITY STATISTICS

CITY OF MELBOURNE MUNICIPALITY POPULATION	98,900
AVERAGE GROSS DENSITY, PEOPLE PER KM² (PER HA)	2,600/KM² (26/HA)
POPULATION GROWTH RATE PER ANNUM	3.28%
COST OF METRO TICKET FOR ONE STOP, € (LOCAL)	€3.20 (A$4)
AVERAGE EARNINGS PER ANNUM, € (LOCAL)	€35,000 (A$45,250)
AVERAGE HOUSE PRICE TO AVERAGE INCOME RATIO	12:1
AVERAGE NUMBER OF CARS PER 1,000 PEOPLE	534

Melbourne has the essence of continental Europe with its vibrant cafe culture within narrow lanes and tree-lined boulevards. Sprawling suburbs, traffic jams and inefficient public transport are irritations for Melbourne residents, yet its diverse cultural scene and innovative architecture put it high on the list of most liveable cities.

Modern Melbourne began as a collection of tents on the banks of the Yarra river in 1835, and the city went through a sustained period of cyclical recession from 1891 before government investment following the second world war introduced a new era of prosperity. By 2000, the government was seeking to restrict new suburban growth to designated growth corridors and encourage high-density living. Melbourne anticipates a greater metropolitan population of 20m by 2050.

Housing Typologies

The majority of dwellings are traditional large detached houses on wide suburban streets. Victorian terraced houses and bungalows in the inner suburbs, built during the 1850's Gold Rush, are becoming increasingly popular. Driven by state initiatives, new sustainable prefabricated homes are appearing around the city.

CASE STUDIES (*interview based)

PROJECT TYPE	ADDRESS	BUILD DATE
* 1 Victorian terrace house	108 Nicholson Street, Fitzroy	1856
* 2 Suburban weatherboard house	41 Hansen Street, Hansen Estate, Footscray	1930
3 Sustainable social housing	K2, Raleigh Street, Windsor	2010
4 High-rise tower	Eureka Tower, 1 Riverside Quay, Southbank	2006
5 Sustainable prefab house, Modscape	Made to order and delivered throughout Australia	–
6 Riverside apartments	New Quay Promenade, Docklands	2002

1 **Victorian Terrace House**

Residents: Tom Keel and family
108 Nicholson Street, Fitzroy

Victorian terrace houses are a ubiquitous part of Melbourne's inner urban streetscape. Tom, who works at home, moved with his family from their large house in the outer suburbs to a more central location three years ago.

Density and urban form
The typical terrace is composed of plots 7 metres wide by 30 metres deep, which are entirely built upon except for a small front yard and private courtyard, giving a relatively high density for a two-storey house.

Flexibility and adaptability
Following renovation, rear access was provided, an apartment above the garage created and living spaces opened up. As mentioned in Chapter 3, each house in what was a terrace of identical houses is now used differently. The combination of their flexibility and central location means that these classic houses, once threatened by demolition, are now much sought after.

Dwelling Plans

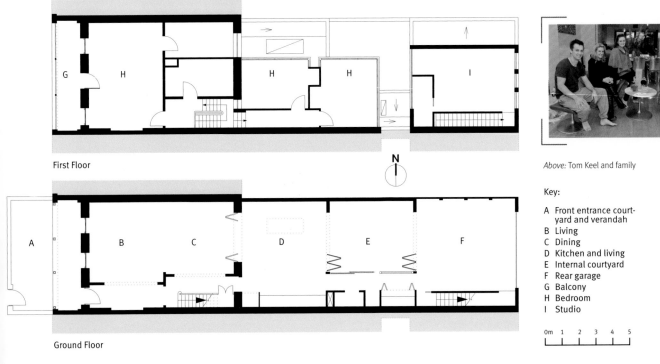

First Floor

N

Ground Floor

Above: Tom Keel and family

Key:

A Front entrance court-
 yard and verandah
B Living
C Dining
D Kitchen and living
E Internal courtyard
F Rear garage
G Balcony
H Bedroom
I Studio

0m 1 2 3 4 5

present but can easily be added. Tom's family walk or cycle to places more frequently than taking the car.

Cost and value

Melbourne is the seventh most expensive city in the world, and the high cost of Nicholson Street does not necessarily reflect the simplicity of construction. Even though Tom's previous house was three times larger and had an immense private garden and an outdoor swimming pool, he considers that his family's quality of life has significantly improved since moving to the centre. University, work, good shops and many facilities can now be reached by bike, and the family are now actively involved in their community ●

Appearance and threshold

The prosperous Victorian Gold Rush ensured that a large number of terraces were built with ornate and elaborate details; characteristic front porches and balconies 'create soft edges,' to use Jan Gehl's expression (see Chapter 4). These provide a private outdoor space, which is nevertheless connected to the life of the street.

Space and light

Tall and generous windows in the front elevation provide plentiful light to the front living area. The courtyard provides the dining and kitchen areas with light and brings together all the common areas of the house. A top-light in the hallway allows daylight into otherwise dark spaces.

Construction and sustainability

Many Victorian-era terraces are built on foundations of bluestone; shared party walls could be built economically and efficiently from local materials. As with many older properties, insulation was not

CASE STUDY DATA

Density (HR/ha):	367
Plot ratio:	1.19:1
Cost to buy:	€5,227/m² (A$6,730/m²)
Buy cost as a multiple of average earnings:	x 39
Floor area:	260m²
Individual plot area:	218m²
Outdoor private amenity space:	38m²
Floor-to-ceiling height:	3m
Floor area per habitable room:	22.5m²
Age of building (and style):	1856, Victorian terraced house
Preferred room in the house:	Open-plan kitchen

SCORES

DENSITY & URBAN FORM	19
FLEXIBILITY & ADAPTABILITY	15
APPEARANCE & THRESHOLD	20
SPACE & LIGHT	17
CONSTRUCTION & SUSTAINABILITY	5
TOTAL	76

Above left: The generous front porch is used extensively throughout the year

Above: The internal courtyard provides light to deep rooms and corridors

Above right: Open-plan living/dining room

2 **Suburban Weatherboard House**

Resident: Mary Olanda

41 Hansen Street, Hansen Estate, Footscray

Weatherboard bungalows from the 1930s populate Footscray, a multicultural suburb. Mary, a university administrator, moved in 23 years ago. The tiny back garden is a source of much pleasure.

Density and urban form

The street follows the typical urban grain of Melbourne. Front gardens and off-street parking produce a low-density neighbourhood, and residents are car-dependent for access to local amenities and the city centre.

Flexibility and adaptability

The house is generous for a single person and large enough for family accommodation. In 2004, the entire timber-frame house was hoisted 300 millimetres towards the rear garden, partition walls reconfigured to create an open-plan layout and living spaces extended 3 metres to the rear.

Above left: Mary in her garden

Above right: The rear porch

Dwelling Plan

Key:

A Bedroom
B Living/Dining/Kitchen
C Garden porch

0m 1 2 3 4 5

SCORES	
DENSITY & URBAN FORM	13
FLEXIBILITY & ADAPTABILITY	10
APPEARANCE & THRESHOLD	15
SPACE & LIGHT	18
CONSTRUCTION & SUSTAINABILITY	11
TOTAL	67

Appearance and threshold

The art deco weatherboard architecture in Footscray was influenced by European immigration during 1920s, and the details of colour and materials vary from house to house. A so-called Nature-strip of identikit trees separates the street from the pavement.

Space and light

The 3-metre-high ceilings and squarely proportioned rooms create a light, spacious and generous interior. Full-height glazing opens the living/kitchen/dining area to the garden.

Construction and sustainability

Made from locally sourced timber, the lightweight sustainable construction is simple to maintain. During the renovation, the walls were insulated with sheep's wool and a reverse-cycle cooling and heating unit installed. Rainwater harvesting complies with Melbourne's water-use target of 150 litres/day.

Cost and value

Following the global trend, Melbourne housing prices peaked in 2008. Mary bought the property in 1989 for $86,000 (€69,500) and spent $100,000 (€81,000) on renovation ●

Above left: Each single storey house has a rear and front garden

Above right: Open plan living, dining and kitchen

CASE STUDY DATA

Density (HR/ha):	114
Plot ratio:	0.35:1
Cost to buy:	€3,590/m² (A$4,435/m²)
Cost to rent/m²	€2.30/m²/m (A$2.90/m²/m)
Buy cost as a multiple of average earnings:	x 12
Floor area:	124m²
Individual plot area:	350m²
Outdoor private amenity space:	110m²
Floor-to-ceiling height:	3m
Floor area per habitable room:	24m²
Age of building (and style):	1930, weatherboard bungalow house
Preferred room in the house:	Living room

3 **Sustainable Social Housing**
K2, Raleigh Street, Windsor 2010

The €25.3m complex, designed by architects Design Inc, consists of 96 units of social housing in four medium-rise buildings. Designed to have a lifespan of 200 years, the K2 Apartments use 55% less mains electricity with photovoltaic and solar-collector areas, 46% less mains supply gas and 53% less mains water than similar-sized apartments. Balcony-accessed units were designed to receive year-round northern sun. Notwithstanding its impeccable sustainability credentials, the development has a brutal and idiosyncratic appearance.

SCORES	
DENSITY & URBAN FORM	6
FLEXIBILITY & ADAPTABILITY	3
APPEARANCE & THRESHOLD	10
SPACE & LIGHT	10
CONSTRUCTION & SUSTAINABILITY	14
TOTAL	43

Public gardens around K2

4 **High-rise Tower**
Eureka Tower, 1 Riverside Quay, Southbank 2006

The second-tallest all-residential building in the world, Eureka Tower was designed by Fender Katsalidis Architects and constructed at a cost of €392m, with gold-plated glass windows on the top 10 floors of the building. It has a total of 92 storeys, with 556 apartments occupying 84 floors and a density of approximately 500HR/ha. The construction was made from a 'Jumpform' system to halve construction time and materials. However, the internal design is inflexible, and the ground floor has little relationship with the surrounding area.

SCORES	
DENSITY & URBAN FORM	4
FLEXIBILITY & ADAPTABILITY	4
APPEARANCE & THRESHOLD	4
SPACE & LIGHT	7
CONSTRUCTION & SUSTAINABILITY	8
TOTAL	27

Eureka Tower

5 **Sustainable Prefab House, Modscape**
Made to order and delivered throughout Australia

Modscape provides modern factory-built modular housing to people with a plot of land or who are looking to extend their existing homes. A Modscape steel-frame home is completed in 12 weeks without the need for additional contractors, and then 'delivered' from its factory in Melbourne. Modules of 4.35 to 15 metres long can be combined in various configurations to suit space and design requirements. Modscape sources environmentally credible materials and those with low embodied energy. Site waste and environmental impact is also reduced as the units are constructed in factory conditions.

Above left: The Modscape unit can be configured to suit different requirements

Left: A unit being constructed within the factory

Above: Interior view

SCORES	
DENSITY & URBAN FORM	8
FLEXIBILITY & ADAPTABILITY	18
APPEARANCE & THRESHOLD	16
SPACE & LIGHT	19
CONSTRUCTION & SUSTAINABILITY	18
TOTAL	79

6 **Riverside Apartments**
New Quay Promenade, Docklands 2002

Situated in a prominent location by the Yarra river, the mid-density apartments are mainly buy-to-let properties, with a high turnover of occupants throughout the year. These apartments achieve a high rental income because of the views across the Yarra river and marina. The forms create good spaces fronting the river, and the open-plan internal layouts enable some flexibility of use. However, there is little sense of community.

SCORES	
DENSITY & URBAN FORM	7
FLEXIBILITY & ADAPTABILITY	5
APPEARANCE & THRESHOLD	7
SPACE & LIGHT	12
CONSTRUCTION & SUSTAINABILITY	1
TOTAL	32

New Quay Promenade

CHAPTER 10

TOKYO

CITY STATISTICS

23 SPECIAL WARDS OF TOKYO POPULATION	8,970,000
AVERAGE GROSS DENSITY, PEOPLE PER KM² (PER HA)	14,400/KM² (144/HA)
POPULATION GROWTH RATE PER ANNUM	0.08%
COST OF METRO TICKET FOR ONE STOP, € (LOCAL)	€1.70 (160 JPY)
AVERAGE EARNINGS PER ANNUM, € (LOCAL)	€71,000 (6,810,000 JPY)
AVERAGE HOUSE PRICE TO AVERAGE INCOME RATIO	19:1
AVERAGE NUMBER OF CARS PER 1000 PEOPLE	743

With 32,450,000 inhabitants, Tokyo is currently the largest metropolitan area in the world. Its train system is arguably the world's most extensive and efficient transportation network, and is key to the city's liveability.

From 1900, Central Tokyo's growth was centred on major railway stations, and the population surged until the Great Kanto Earthquake of 1923, which killed 140,000 and ravaged large parts of the timber-structured city. Second world war air raids destroyed most of the remaining traditional urban housing stock. These two catastrophes fundamentally changed the Japanese attitude to house-building and homes.

By the 1980s' Tokyo was economically successful and one of the densest cities in the world; 26% of the Japanese population now live in Tokyo and there is strong support for decentralisation–, particularly in light of the 2011 earthquake and tsunami, which brought Tokyo to a standstill. Today Tokyo has to deal with the problems associated with a declining and ageing urban population and a high proportion of single dwellers, from college students to the widowed elderly.

Housing Typologies

Multi-unit residential complexes and condensed suburban developments of detached mini-houses are the predominant forms of housing in Tokyo, together with one-room studio apartments in both high-rise and low-rise forms. Intense mixed-use areas dominated by shopping, such as Roppongi Hills and Tokyo Midtown, reflect Tokyo's early 21st-century boom era.

'Japan lives with drastic segregation between the sublime, the ugly, and the utterly without qualities. Dominance of the last two categories makes mere presence of the first stunning: when beauty "happens", it is absolutely surprising.' [1]

1   Rem Koolhaas, Learning Japanese, S,M,L,XL, New York, The Monacelli Press, 1995

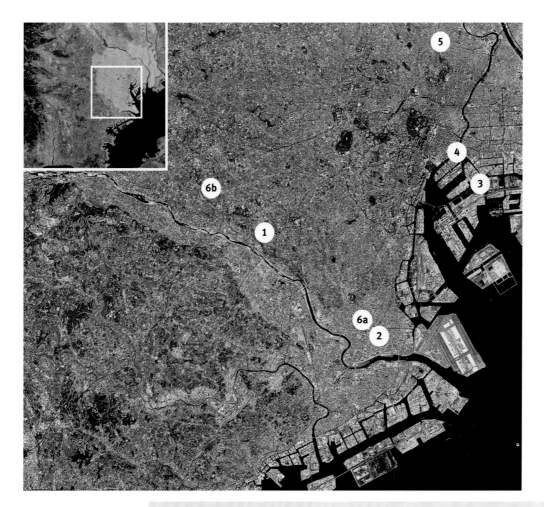

CASE STUDIES (*interview based)

	PROJECT TYPE	ADDRESS	BUILD DATE
* 1	3LDK apartment conversion	3–16 Kaminoge, Setagawa-ku	1971
* 2	Sekisui Heim prefabricated house	Ota-ku	
3	Shinonome housing project	Tōkyō-to, Kōtō-ku, Shinonome	2003
4	High rise	Century Park Tower, River City 21, Tsukuda, Cuo-ku	1999
5	Traditional Tokyo housing	Yanaka, Edo-period style	1900s
6	(a) Moriyama house	Tōkyō-to, Ota-ku, Nishikamata	2005
	(b) United Cubes: Seijo Garden Courts	5 Seijo, Setagaya-ku, Tōkyō-to	2007

Dwelling Plan

Key:

A Entrance and shoe storage
B Bedroom
C Dining
D Living
E Balcony
F Tatami room
G Kitchen
H Bathroom

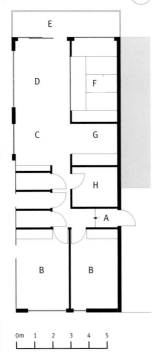

0m 1 2 3 4 5

1 **3LDK Apartment Conversion**

Residents: Toshihiro and Yumiko Okamoto
3–16 Kaminoge, Setagawa-ku

Toshihiro and his wife, Yumiko, a journalist and a fashion director, live in an apartment situated 20 minutes from Tokyo's transport hub, Shibuya station. 3LDK (living/dining/kitchen and three rooms) is local property-speak for the configuration of this flat. The building is 40 years old and was previously an international school, so it could be considered historical housing by Tokyo's standards. New constructions usually replace buildings older than 15 years.

Density and urban form

They live on the second floor of one of three seven-storey monolithic high-density blocks. The block is not typical for Tokyo, but it sits comfortably within the urban grain. The high-density area immediately surrounding Kaminoge station is filled with shops and services. Community block meetings are held every month. High parking fees of 50,000 JPY (€455) per month discourage car ownership.

Flexibility and adaptability

The apartment contains a 13-square-metre (or 4 tsubo) tatami room, a unique form of flexible space that adapts to their needs: a place to have a nap or read or to use as a guest bedroom. The original structure proved to be suitable for conversion, with its simple clear-span frame.

Above: The living room

Left: Toshihiro and Yumiko

Opposite right: A single step delineates the threshold

Opposite far right: The tiered terraces

Appearance and threshold
The block is out of character with the area, which is composed mainly of small detached houses. The grounds are semi-public but accommodate only car parking and have no real social function. Balconies overlook the street, contributing something to the public realm.

Space and light
Situated at the block end, the apartment has north-, west- and east-facing windows, enabling light to enter most of the house. The low ceiling height, use of colour and detail, and wide open plan emphasise horizontal living, and Toshihiro and Yumiko like the way that it corresponds to the typical Japanese way of life. The apartment is large for Tokyo's space standards: an average size home in Tokyo is 64.5 square metres (although the average size across Japan is 92 square metres).

Construction and sustainability
The building is of precast concrete construction with large balconies and full-height glazed windows facing onto the street, but it does not incorporate any sustainable technology.

Cost and value
This multistorey block is an anomaly in Setagawa but it is inexpensive relative to the size and quality of the space, which distinguishes it from the more expensive small generic new-build flats that are widely available ●

CASE STUDY DATA

Density (HR/ha):	648
Plot ratio:	1.6:1
Cost to buy:	€3,450/m² (383,333 JPY/m²)
Cost to rent/m²	€13/m²/m (1,458 JPY/m²/m)
Buy cost as a multiple of average earnings:	x 5.5
Floor area:	96m²
Plot area:	3,700m²
Outdoor private amenity space:	8.4m²
Floor-to-ceiling height:	2m
Floor area per habitable room:	16m²
Age of building (and style):	1971, low-rise apartment block
Preferred room in the house:	Living/dining room

SCORES

DENSITY & URBAN FORM	9
FLEXIBILITY & ADAPTABILITY	10
APPEARANCE & THRESHOLD	7
SPACE & LIGHT	13
CONSTRUCTION & SUSTAINABILITY	4
TOTAL	43

G   G

G

I   G

First Floor

D   E

C

B   A   F

Ground Floor

Dwelling Plans

Key:

A Entrance and shoe storage
B Kitchen
C Dining
D Living
E Tatami room
F Bathroom
G Bedroom
I Ensuite room

0m 1 2 3 4 5

2 Sekisui Heim Prefabricated House
Ota-ku

On the basis of the high demand for affordable urban accommodation in the 1950s, large national construction companies geared up to deliver an estimated 4m homes quickly and efficiently. Today, they dominate the Japanese housing market. Sekisui Heim produces 10 modular dwelling units a day in factory conditions, delivering some 2,000 homes a year.

Density and urban form
The most popular unit size is a detached house of 115 square metres over two storeys and typically erected on a plot only nominally larger than the house, resulting in relatively high densities for low-rise communities. The culture of constructing individual houses without party walls is wasteful in terms of both space and energy; nevertheless, most new Japanese houses are constructed on individual plots.

Flexibility and adaptability
All domestic layouts are based on a central living area (a living/ dining/ kitchen – LDK), with a tatami room and private rooms. The Sekisui Heim box-frame structure is made from 10-square-metre modules; the buyer chooses from an array of layout options to suit the site, allowing large open-plan (up to 50 square metres) and double-height spaces.

Appearance and threshold
Despite the highly sophisticated methods of construction, the end product is mundane-looking; curiously, maintenance takes preference over aesthetics for a product with an average life of 20 years. Factory-applied stack-bond ceramic tiles are used as waterproof cladding and require minimum maintenance.

Space and light

A catalogue of house types gives customers their choice of interior styles and window layouts. The show home we visited had glazing on all sides of the detached house, so light was able to penetrate into the core of the dwelling.

Construction and sustainability

A total of 80% of the structure is assembled in the factory, reducing site waste and streamlining the building process as well as reducing carbon emissions. The steel frame is engineered to address Japanese building codes for earthquakes, typhoons and fire-retardance performance. The unit incorporates sustainable technology, including a heat exchange ventilation system. While the shell can be erected in five hours, it takes one month to fit out. Tokyo's 'demolish and rebuild' practice produces thousands of tonnes of waste each year, but Sekisui Heim reuses steel frames and offers a discount on a new home when an existing structure is traded in.

Cost and value

Tokyo's turbulent history is a contributing factor to the Japanese attitude to property, which looks upon building construction as a disposable commodity. Although the land holds value, the building value typically decreases to nil after 15 years. Generations of families replace their houses on the same plot, so driving the house-building economy ●

SCORES	
DENSITY & URBAN FORM	14
FLEXIBILITY & ADAPTABILITY	12
APPEARANCE & THRESHOLD	8
SPACE & LIGHT	12
CONSTRUCTION & SUSTAINABILITY	17
TOTAL	**63**

Left: A Sekisui Heim worker in front of the show home

Right above: Mini-houses in a typical Tokyo street

Right below: Open and bright interiors within the show home

CASE STUDY DATA

Density (HR/ha):	777
Plot ratio:	1.27:1
Cost to buy:	€2,645/m² (270,000 JPY/m²) *
Buy cost as a multiple of average earnings:	x 4.6 (excluding land costs)
Floor area:	115m² **
Plot area:	90m²
Outdoor private amenity space:	15m²
Floor-to-ceiling height:	2.5m
Floor area per habitable room:	9.5m²
Age of building (and style):	Made-to-order prefabricated house

★   Based on a popular Sekisui Heim house type
★★   Based on government-designated plot ratios and popular Sekisui Heim house types

Shinonome Court Project

3 Shinonome Housing Project
Tōkyō-to, Kōtō-ku, Shinonome 2003

Shinonome Court Project sits in a reclaimed seabed area of Tokyo Bay. It is a multi-family housing project of 420 housing units, designed by various notable architects, of single-storey and duplex apartments, some of which contain a separate flexible 25-square-metre 'neutral' zone. Wide corridors open up to semi-private foyers and double-height private gardens, and blocks are linked by a main pedestrian street that connects the internal ground-floor services – kindergarten, playgrounds, shops and offices – with the riverside park at its ends.

SCORES	
DENSITY & URBAN FORM	9
FLEXIBILITY & ADAPTABILITY	6
APPEARANCE & THRESHOLD	11
SPACE & LIGHT	11
CONSTRUCTION & SUSTAINABILITY	5
TOTAL	42

4 High Rise
Century Park Tower, River City 21, Tsukuda, Cuo-ku 1999

This flat is in one of a series of uniformly detailed residential tower blocks, 54 storeys high, built on a former industrial site overlooking Tokyo Bay, but the lack of shared communal space, the anonymous internal corridors and cramped inflexible flats reduce the scheme's appeal.

SCORES	
DENSITY & URBAN FORM	4
FLEXIBILITY & ADAPTABILITY	4
APPEARANCE & THRESHOLD	2
SPACE & LIGHT	3
CONSTRUCTION & SUSTAINABILITY	3
TOTAL	16

Century Park Tower in context

Timber shophouses provide human-scale spaces

Traditional Japanese temples offer tranquility

5 **Traditional Tokyo Housing**
Yanaka, Edo-period style 1900s

Pockets of traditional Japanese wooden-construction buildings still exist in Tokyo. These districts are resilient and adaptable to change and display a strong sense of community, with small-scale commerce and vibrant street life.

SCORES	
DENSITY & URBAN FORM	19
FLEXIBILITY & ADAPTABILITY	14
APPEARANCE & THRESHOLD	20
SPACE & LIGHT	12
CONSTRUCTION & SUSTAINABILITY	9
TOTAL	74

6 (a) **Moriyama House**
Tōkyō-to, Ota-ku, Nishikamata 2005

Moriyama House by SANAA is a modern interpretation of the Japanese suburban plot and is composed of white cuboids with loadbearing walls only 6 centimetres thick reinforced with steel plates, allowing large window openings. Five compact rental apartments, of between 16 and 30 square metres, are dispersed into 10 separate buildings in a semi-private landscape. Every person has their own room and there is one unit which acts as the shared living room.

(b) **United Cubes: Seijo Garden Courts**
5 Seijo, Setagaya-ku, Tōkyō-to 2007

United Cubes by SANAA, with its simple pale-brick facades, follows a similar aesthetic principle, but the dwellings are more integrated, internal spaces are more generous, and large sliding glazed partitions open up to private courtyards.

SCORES	
DENSITY & URBAN FORM	16
FLEXIBILITY & ADAPTABILITY	12
APPEARANCE & THRESHOLD	16
SPACE & LIGHT	17
CONSTRUCTION & SUSTAINABILITY	10
TOTAL	71

Left: Moriyama House in context
Right: Semi-private entrance in United Cubes

CHAPTER 11

LONDON

CITY STATISTICS

GREATER LONDON: 33 BOROUGHS POPULATION	8,200,000
AVERAGE GROSS DENSITY, PEOPLE PER KM² (PER HA)	5,220/KM² (52/HA)
POPULATION GROWTH RATE PER ANNUM	0.92%
COST OF METRO TICKET FOR ONE STOP, € (LOCAL)	€5.50 (£4.30)
AVERAGE EARNINGS PER ANNUM, € (LOCAL)	€39,300 (£30,800)
AVERAGE HOUSE PRICE TO AVERAGE INCOME RATIO	15:1
AVERAGE NUMBER OF CARS PER 1,000 PEOPLE	225

A world creative, financial and political centre, London is a collection of multicultural urban villages with at least 50 non-indigenous communities. While it has some of the highest property values in the world, it has 13 out of 20 of the most deprived wards in the country.

Roman Londinium grew organically until the Great Fire of London in 1666 destroyed about 60% of the urban fabric, prompting the Rebuilding of London Act which established brick as the predominant structural material. Despite Christopher Wren's attempts to replan London, the city was rebuilt in its original organic pattern. The Act standardised the sizes of rooms and layouts, and four rates of houses were specified; the grand and most expensive First Rate Houses occupied plot areas of over 80 square metres. Fourth Rate houses were the cheapest and smallest dwellings, which occupied a less than 30-square-metre plot area.

With the introduction of railways during the Industrial Revolution, wealthier classes moved to the rural suburbs, leaving behind inner-city slums. Following the second world war, local authorities rebuilt war-torn areas with high-rise blocks, often now unpopular and ill-maintained.

The 2011 London Plan has set out targets for affordable, sustainable communities, including an aspiration to create more than 200,000 new homes in the Thames Gateway over the next 15 to 20 years.

Housing Typologies

London is predominantly low rise, with many local communities centred on tube or train stations and 18th- and 19th-century family holdings encompassing the most valuable real estate. Contained by the Green Belt, a 30-kilometre band of two- and three-storey Victorian and Georgian terraces, postwar housing and the latest multistorey idiosyncratic additions encircles Central London.

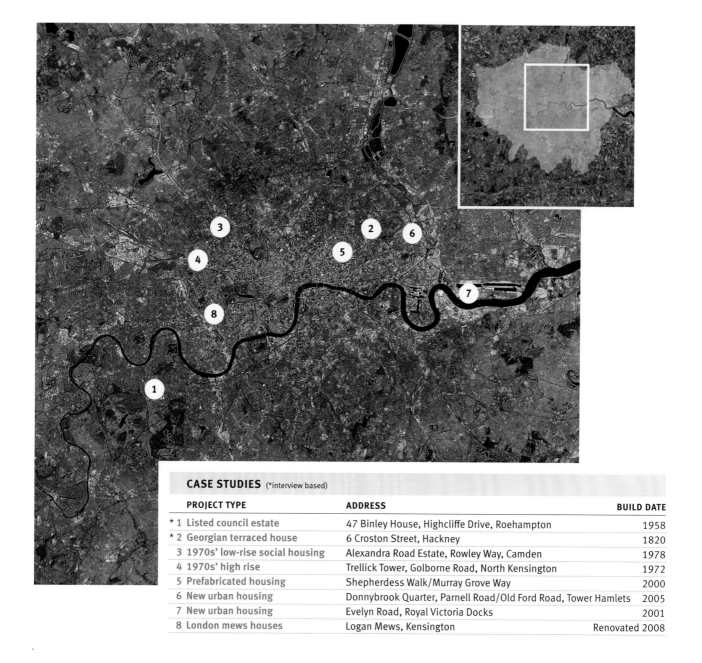

CASE STUDIES (*interview based)

	PROJECT TYPE	ADDRESS	BUILD DATE
* 1	Listed council estate	47 Binley House, Highcliffe Drive, Roehampton	1958
* 2	Georgian terraced house	6 Croston Street, Hackney	1820
3	1970s' low-rise social housing	Alexandra Road Estate, Rowley Way, Camden	1978
4	1970s' high rise	Trellick Tower, Golborne Road, North Kensington	1972
5	Prefabricated housing	Shepherdess Walk/Murray Grove Way	2000
6	New urban housing	Donnybrook Quarter, Parnell Road/Old Ford Road, Tower Hamlets	2005
7	New urban housing	Evelyn Road, Royal Victoria Docks	2001
8	London mews houses	Logan Mews, Kensington	Renovated 2008

1 Listed Council Estate

Resident: Irina Nazarenko
47 Binley House, Highcliffe Drive, Roehampton

Binley House is one of four linear concrete blocks surrounded by parkland – a direct translation of Le Corbusier's Unité d'Habitation and Ville Radieuse (radiant city) concepts. Irina bought her two-bed duplex apartment in 2000 and has lived there since with her daughter.

Density and urban form

The high-rise linear block set in semi-public parkland achieves a relatively low density, and while the open space provides beautiful views it has no other urban function. The dwellings are detached from main street activities, and Irina comments that the level of petty crime and violence has increased as the original tenants from 1954 have moved out.

Flexibility and adaptability

The simple internal layout works well; however, the rooms are cramped and the lack of storage compromises the apartment's flexibility. Although the maisonette format gives the flat some interest, there is little opportunity to change the basic plan format. Irina has recently converted one of the bedrooms into a home office.

Irina in front of her apartment

Dwelling Plans

Key:

A Hallway
B Kitchen
C Living
D Balcony
E Home Office
F Bedroom

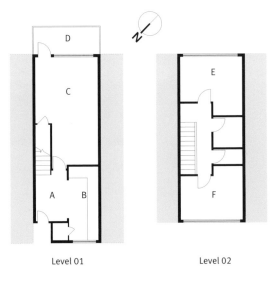

Level 01

Level 02

0m 1 2 3 4 5

Appearance and threshold

The four Unité blocks sit attractively in the surrounding parkland. The buildings are handsome if brutal objects designed to exacting proportions, but the experience of entering through an undercroft, communal lifts and open-access balconies is somewhat alienating.

Space and light

The cross section with balcony access provides dual aspect, and the views are spectacular, contributing to a sense of space within the flat. But the floor area falls well below the London Design Guide standards for a two-bedroom flat. The 5-square-metre balcony provides a welcome private outdoor space.

Construction and sustainability

The cladding employs some precast concrete, but the primary structure was constructed in situ. As with other buildings of the period, there have been problems with cold bridging, water ingress and condensation.

Cost and value

In our opinion, the additional capital cost of creating a heavy concrete frame is not justified when compared with simple low-rise construction of a similar density. However, the apartments are now affordable at 4.5 times the average salary, and are cheaper than other homes in the locality ●

SCORES	
DENSITY & URBAN FORM	3
FLEXIBILITY & ADAPTABILITY	6
APPEARANCE & THRESHOLD	7
SPACE & LIGHT	12
CONSTRUCTION & SUSTAINABILITY	4
TOTAL	32

Top left: Binley House, Roehampton

Top right: The buildings are detached from the ground and from the street

Below: Living room

CASE STUDY DATA	
Density (HR/ha):	400
Plot ratio:	0.9:1
Cost to buy:	€2,740/m² (£2,258/m²)
Cost to rent/m²	€17.50/m²/m (£14.50/m²/m)
Buy cost as a multiple of average earnings:	x 4.5
Floor area:	62m²
Plot area:	6,600m²
Outdoor private amenity space:	5.1m²
Floor-to-ceiling height:	2.4m
Floor area per habitable room:	13m²
Age of building (and style):	1958, Brutalist slab blocks
Preferred room in the house:	Living room

2 **Georgian Terraced House**
Residents: Justin and Sam
6 Croston Street, Hackney

This Georgian terraced house is located close to Broadway Market, an area made up of many diverse communities, and Justin and Sam bought their house 16 years ago.

Density and urban form
The house is two storeys above ground, but includes a basement that opens on to a large garden. Density is relatively high for a modest-looking dwelling. One end of the street is closed, creating a cul-de-sac, and this increases the sense of community.

Flexibility and adaptability
The Croston Street houses were built for City of London clerks, but each was swiftly adapted to accommodate three families, one per

Sam, Justin and the kids

Georgian terraced houses

Dwelling Plans

Key:

A Rear garden
B Living with rooflight above
C Dining
D Kitchen
E Front lightwell
F Utility room
G Lower hall
H Bedroom
I   Study
J   Main entrance

0m 1 2 3 4 5

First Floor

Ground Floor

Lower-Ground Floor

floor, with a shared washroom in the garden. The Georgian house is a flexible housing form, and Justin and Sam have been altering the layout since they moved in.

Appearance and threshold
Each house has a stepped entrance between the light-well railings and the brick facades. Arched windows and symmetrical frontages create a well-proportioned facade, with paired gables increasing the grandeur of a modest terrace. The group of properties was emergency-listed in the 1980s.

Space and light
The lower ground floor is bright and generous, and glazed sliding doors to the garden create a bright, spacious, open-plan interior enhanced by roof lighting. Being a 'Fourth Rate' Georgian house, habitable spaces are relatively small and ceiling heights relatively low. The loft provides valuable storage space, with additional storage in the new extension.

Construction and sustainability
The bricks were made from site clay excavated to create the lower-ground space, and flexible lime mortar has contributed to their longevity. Floors and roofs are constructed of timber, and a central spine wall, separating the stairwell from the habitable spaces, supports the structure.

Cost and value
Justin and Sam bought their house for a tenth of its current value, and houses in the area, with their authentic appearance and flexible layouts, have become sought after and expensive.

Georgian Houses in London
The grander First Rate houses in, for instance, Bedford Square share many of the characteristics of the modest Fourth Rate houses near Broadway Market. Simple economic construction, flexible interior space and attractive proportions are common features but First Rate properties are more generous in their dimensions, allowing conversion to hotels, offices and university departments ●

SCORES	
DENSITY & URBAN FORM	19
FLEXIBILITY & ADAPTABILITY	17
APPEARANCE & THRESHOLD	20
SPACE & LIGHT	15
CONSTRUCTION & SUSTAINABILITY	4
TOTAL	75

Top: The basement level has been opened up to create a large, flexible family space

Above left: Large windows provide plentiful light to the bedrooms

Above right: Bedford Square

CASE STUDY DATA	
Density (HR/ha):	357
Plot ratio:	0.82:1
Cost to buy:	€7,225/m² (£5,910/m²)
Buy cost as a multiple of average earnings:	x 26.5
Floor area:	138m²
Plot area:	168m²
Outdoor private amenity space:	84m²
Floor-to-ceiling height:	Basement 2.1m, GF 2.4m, 1st F 2.25m
Floor area per habitable room:	14m²
Age of building (and style):	1820, Georgian worker's cottage
Preferred room in the house:	Kitchen and living room

3 **1970s' Low-rise Social Housing**
Alexandra Road Estate, Rowley Way,
Camden 1978

The Grade II-listed Alexandra Road Estate
was designed by Neave Brown. It contains
520 apartments arranged in four-storey
terraces and includes a school, community
centre and parkland, but the buildings
are not integrated into the surrounding
neighbourhood. The interior spaces are
bright and generous, but because of the
expensive site-cast reinforced concrete
construction the housing model is
unrepeatable.

SCORES	
DENSITY & URBAN FORM	12
FLEXIBILITY & ADAPTABILITY	5
APPEARANCE & THRESHOLD	12
SPACE & LIGHT	12
CONSTRUCTION & SUSTAINABILITY	0
TOTAL	41

High-level street in Alexandra Road Estate

4 **1970s' High Rise**
Trellick Tower, Golborne Road,
North Kensington 1972

Trellick Tower, of the same era, was Ernö
Goldfinger's interpretation of the Ville
Radieuse concept on a constricted inner-city
site. Thirty-one storeys contain nine different
types of large flats and maisonettes that
are accessed by an anonymous car park,
entrances and external walkways. The public
spaces are brutal in design, and security
cameras cover neglected and isolated areas.
The residents' association has enabled a
sense of community in the high rise, and the
apartments have increased in popularity in
recent years.

SCORES	
DENSITY & URBAN FORM	4
FLEXIBILITY & ADAPTABILITY	7
APPEARANCE & THRESHOLD	6
SPACE & LIGHT	15
CONSTRUCTION & SUSTAINABILITY	1
TOTAL	33

Trellick Tower

Murray Grove

5 **Prefabricated Housing**
Shepherdess Walk/Murray Grove Way
2000

The prefabricated construction, designed by Cartwright Pickard, provides a relatively high-density scheme of 30 one-and two-bedroom flats. Habitable rooms overlook the semi-private gardens, and outdoor gantries separate the flats from street activity. Preassembled bathroom units contributed to efficient and economic construction. Flexibility and adaptability of use are absent.

SCORES	
DENSITY & URBAN FORM	10
FLEXIBILITY & ADAPTABILITY	6
APPEARANCE & THRESHOLD	15
SPACE & LIGHT	11
CONSTRUCTION & SUSTAINABILITY	11
TOTAL	53

6 New Urban Housing
Donnybrook Quarter, Parnell Road/Old Ford Road, Tower Hamlets 2005

This is a competition-winning scheme, commissioned by Peabody Trust, for affordable accommodation. Donnybrook Quarter by Peter Barber Architects, is a fairly dense mixed-use scheme consisting of dwelling units as well as community, work and retail spaces. The three-storey blocks are configured in a terrace and courtyard typology that creates a semi-public threshold. In contrast to Copenhagen's Potato Rows, the streets are unoccupied, with a lack of street life, furniture and planting.

SCORES	
DENSITY & URBAN FORM	15
FLEXIBILITY & ADAPTABILITY	10
APPEARANCE & THRESHOLD	17
SPACE & LIGHT	14
CONSTRUCTION & SUSTAINABILITY	4
TOTAL	60

Above: Donnybrook Quarter: competition visual by Peter Barber Architects

Right: Internal street in Donnybrook Quarter

7 New Urban Housing
Evelyn Road, Royal Victoria Docks 2001

Evelyn Road by Niall McLaughlin consists of 12 two-bedroom apartments within two low-rise blocks. The iridescent-film facade creates an interesting relationship with the street, but large staggered windows do not appear to supply sufficient light to the principal rooms. The building shell is well insulated and residents claim that the interior spaces tend to overheat during hot summers. The apartments meet London Housing Design Guide standards. Although medium density, the scheme is configured as flats with shared access staircases rather than as a flexible terraced houses with front doors.

SCORES	
DENSITY & URBAN FORM	12
FLEXIBILITY & ADAPTABILITY	9
APPEARANCE & THRESHOLD	17
SPACE & LIGHT	9
CONSTRUCTION & SUSTAINABILITY	12
TOTAL	59

Far left: Irredescent facades of Evelyn Road

Left: Evelyn Road: large spaces with small windows

8 London Mews Houses
Logan Mews, Kensington Renovated 2008

Nineteenth-century mews houses built as staff quarters and stables for the nearby town houses are concentrated in some of the most expensive parts of London. This modest two-storey housing type has increased in popularity as a flexible housing form, and is usually configured in high-density clusters on narrow cobbled streets that provide separation from the surrounding busy main thoroughfares. In many cases these houses have undergone multiple conversions, from stables to commercial premises to residences.

SCORES	
DENSITY & URBAN FORM	20
FLEXIBILITY & ADAPTABILITY	15
APPEARANCE & THRESHOLD	18
SPACE & LIGHT	15
CONSTRUCTION & SUSTAINABILITY	4
TOTAL	72

Mews house, Kensington

CHAPTER 12

NEW YORK

CITY STATISTICS

NEW YORK CITY: 5 BOROUGHS POPULATION	8,245,000
AVERAGE GROSS DENSITY, PEOPLE PER KM² (PER HA)	10,440/KM² (104/HA)
POPULATION GROWTH RATE PER ANNUM	0.85%
COST OF METRO TICKET FOR ONE STOP, € (LOCAL)	€2 (US$2.50)
AVERAGE EARNINGS PER ANNUM, € (LOCAL)	€25,200 (US$31,000)
AVERAGE HOUSE PRICE TO AVERAGE INCOME RATIO	11:1
AVERAGE NUMBER OF CARS PER 1,000 PEOPLE	472

New York has been dramatically transformed over the last three decades. During the 1970s' whole neighbourhoods emptied as the city declined with crime and grime; but today, with new parks and public spaces, it approximates Jane Jacobs's aspirations as a dense, community-centred city, and has become a desirable place to live.

New York grew in importance as a trading port, and was the capital of the US from 1785 until 1790. The Commissioners' Plan of 1811 expanded the city street grid to encompass all of Manhattan.

The 1904 subway helped to bind together the modern city of New York. In the early 1930s the landmark Chrysler and Empire State buildings were developed, immigrants lived in overcrowded tenements and the metropolitan population exceeded 10 million. Today, the city is a major global financial and industrial centre composed of five boroughs – Manhattan, the Bronx, Brooklyn, Queens and Staten Island – with hundreds of distinct neighbourhoods.

Housing Typologies

New York has a large collection of residential towers dating from the 1930s. However, the brownstone town houses and tenements define the character of the city's residential districts. Densely populated neighbourhoods in the Bronx and Brooklyn feature single-family dwellings and two-family houses in various architectural styles. Former industrial warehouses are now popular mixed-use residences. Larger detached houses are found in the suburbs of the city.

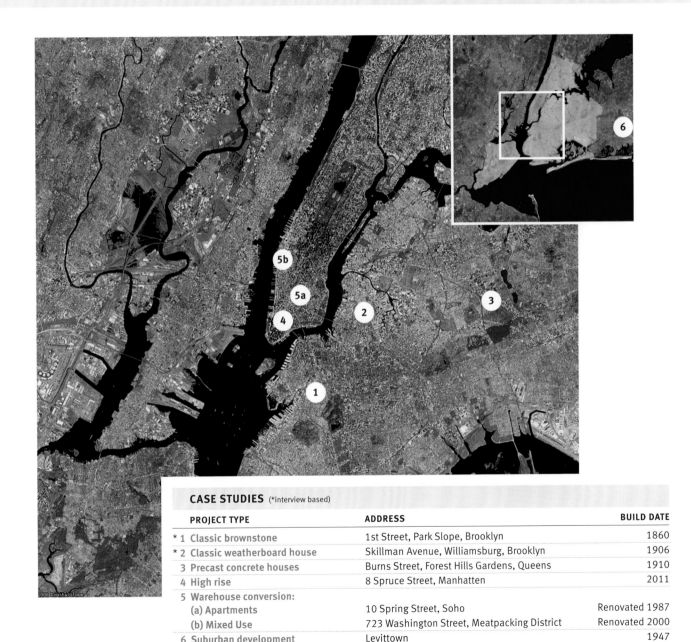

CASE STUDIES (*interview based)

	PROJECT TYPE	ADDRESS	BUILD DATE
* 1	Classic brownstone	1st Street, Park Slope, Brooklyn	1860
* 2	Classic weatherboard house	Skillman Avenue, Williamsburg, Brooklyn	1906
3	Precast concrete houses	Burns Street, Forest Hills Gardens, Queens	1910
4	High rise	8 Spruce Street, Manhatten	2011
5	Warehouse conversion:		
	(a) Apartments	10 Spring Street, Soho	Renovated 1987
	(b) Mixed Use	723 Washington Street, Meatpacking District	Renovated 2000
6	Suburban development	Levittown	1947

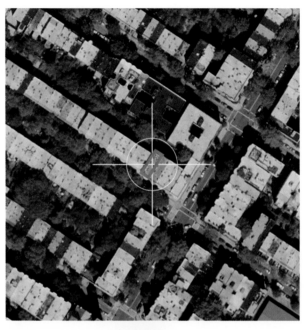

1 **Classic brownstone**
Residents: Julia and family
1st Street, Park Slope, Brooklyn

Brownstone row houses dominate Park Slope and afford residents a community-based lifestyle with urban density. Good schools, low crime, large green spaces, excellent services and shops attracted Julia and her husband to rent a fourth-floor apartment. New Yorkers consider this to be the most liveable neighbourhood in the city, but the area falls short on affordability and diversity.

Density and urban form
The brownstone typology is typically composed of four- to five-storey blocks (including basement) with rear gardens: originally single houses, but which typically now accommodate four apartments per plot. This urban form achieves very high densities in mid-rise dwellings, and wide tree-lined streets connect to large parks.

Flexibility and adaptability
A majority of the townhouses in Park Slope have been converted with relative ease from spacious single-family dwellings into apartments, as the principal stairwell is separate from the habitable

Julia's brownstone house in Park Slope

Dwelling Plans

Key:

A Apartment entrance
B Bedroom
C Kitchen
D Dining/living
E Stair to roof terrace
F Roof terrace

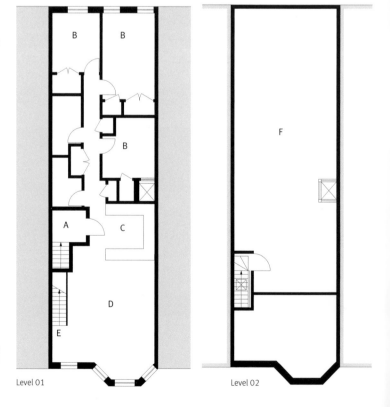

0m   1   2   3   4   5

Level 01   Level 02

rooms. The deep plots allow internal flexibility and the flat roofs provide opportunities to extend.

Appearance and threshold
Brownstone houses were based on the classic US Federal and Revivalist styles. The high ceilings and tall bay windows elaborate the rusticated stone facade, and the lines of mature grown trees soften the ambience along the wide streets. The steps up to the large entrance provide a degree of separation from casual street activities.

Space and light
Mid-storey-height blocks and wide streets enable light to access the front and rear rooms of each apartment floor. Julia's south-facing open-plan kitchen/living room gains natural light through tall sash windows while small light wells, situated in the centre of each plot, provide inadequate light to the small bedroom. The raised ground-floor level enables light to access the habitable basement rooms.

Construction and sustainability
Brownstone houses were constructed of brick and clad in Portland brownstone, which decreased construction costs. During the late 1800s' brownstone was readily available and could be shipped easily to New York from neighbouring Connecticut and New Jersey.

Like a majority of Park Slope's residents, Julia and her husband work, shop and eat nearby and have little need for a car. Local shops and amenities are sustained by the high-density community.

Cost and value
A Park Slope home that cost $300,000 a decade ago now sells for $1.3 million; houses cost 45.28% more than the median sales price in the general Brooklyn area. The historical value, generously proportioned rooms and private outdoor space offered by brownstone row houses make for the most sought-after accommodation ●

SCORES

DENSITY & URBAN FORM	20
FLEXIBILITY & ADAPTABILITY	15
APPEARANCE & THRESHOLD	19
SPACE & LIGHT	18
CONSTRUCTION & SUSTAINABILITY	2
TOTAL	74

CASE STUDY DATA

Density (HR/ha):	926
Plot ratio:	2.36:1
Cost to buy:	€9,165/m² ($12,255/m²)
Cost to rent:	€25/m²/m ($34/m²/m)
Buy cost as a multiple of average earnings:	x 40
Floor area:	102m²
Plot area:	216m²
Outdoor private amenity space:	87m²
Floor-to-ceiling height:	2.5m
Floor area per habitable room:	13.4m²
Age of building (and style):	1860, Federal style
Preferred room in the house:	Kitchen and roof terrace

Above: Julia and her son

Below: The roof terrace overlooks Manhatten

2 **Classic Weatherboard House**
Residents: O and Peter
Skillman Avenue, Williamsburg, Brooklyn

As areas such as SoHo and the East Village became gentrified in the 1970s, artists moved to the light industrial area of Williamsburg. O and Peter are both artists and were drawn to the area by the low property prices and convenient transportation. Today the ethnically diverse, densely populated neighbourhood is being redefined by rapid development of housing and retail space.

Density and urban form
The two-storey house is situated in a narrow plot between three- and four-storey houses. Buildings of varying heights occupy separate plots and have small front porches and rear gardens that create a medium-density neighbourhood.

Flexibility and adaptability
O and Peter have divided the front and back of the property laterally so that they can rent out the front apartment and live in the rear one. Both of them work from home. Peter's studio is the garden shed, and the first floor belongs to O, with their bedroom on the ground floor.

Appearance and threshold
A simple and handsome facade also allows options for subdivision internally. The 2.5m zone in front of the house provides a soft separation from the street. Each house on Skillman Avenue has a uniquely different elevational treatment using brick or timber. Varying house heights and different finishes enliven the street scene.

Space and light
Dividing the house into two apartments limits usable space, but clever use of mirrors enlarges the sense of the open-plan area and elegantly connects the small spaces. The rear elevation is entirely glazed, connecting the living room to the garden and with south-facing full-height glazing giving light into the kitchen and bedroom.

Construction and sustainability
The timber-frame construction is sustainable, lightweight and simple to erect. O and Peter can maintain their property themselves and, being close to the metro, do not require a car.

Cost and value
What were once low rents have now increased since the mid 1990s, driving out the creative communities. Average rents in Williamsburg range from approximately $1,400 for a studio apartment to $2,600–4,000 for a two-bedroom apartment ●

Top: O and Peter in their garden

Above: The living room/kitchen opens to the garden

Ground Floor   First Floor

0m 1   2   3   4   5

O's studio

Dwelling Plans

Key:

A Front porch, bike and refuse storage
B Entrance to front apartment
C Side entrance to rear apartment
D Studio workshop
E Kitchen
F Living
G Bedroom
H Studio
J Garden

O and Peter's house

SCORES

DENSITY & URBAN FORM	18
FLEXIBILITY & ADAPTABILITY	17
APPEARANCE & THRESHOLD	20
SPACE & LIGHT	11
CONSTRUCTION & SUSTAINABILITY	6
TOTAL	72

CASE STUDY DATA

Density (HR/ha):	198
Plot ratio:	0.5:1
Cost to buy:	€4,980/m² ($6,400/m²)
Buy cost as a multiple of average earnings:	x 39
Floor area:	125m²
Plot area:	252m²
Outdoor private amenity space:	85m²
Floor-to-ceiling height:	GF 2.5m, 1st F 2.2m
Floor area per habitable room:	17m²
Age of building (and style):	1906, weatherboard house
Preferred room in the house:	The glazed extension

A Tudor-style precast house

3 Precast Concrete Houses
Burns Street, Forest Hills Gardens,
Queens 1910

Forest Hills Gardens is based upon
Ebenezer Howard's Garden City concept,
which celebrated low-density detached
dwellings in large grounds with winding
roads to reduce traffic. The detached
houses, built of precast concrete from
1910, are innovative even by today's
standards, but appear as traditional English
village dwellings (see Chapter 6). Today, the
area contains some of the most expensive
housing in New York City.

SCORES	
DENSITY & URBAN FORM	15
FLEXIBILITY & ADAPTABILITY	5
APPEARANCE & THRESHOLD	11
SPACE & LIGHT	13
CONSTRUCTION & SUSTAINABILITY	12
TOTAL	56

4 High Rise
8 Spruce Street, Manhatten 2011

'New York by Gehry', a 76-storey tower
completed in 2011, contains 903 luxury
apartments. Frank Gehry's distinctive
aesthetic cuts a glamorous figure on the
Manhattan skyline, with undulating waves
of stainless steel intended to reflect the
changing light. However, the interiors
are small and generic. A majority of the
dwellings do not have private amenity
space. Three centrally located floors are set
aside for resident-only social amenities;
the lowest six floors house a public school
and one floor is for New York City Hospital.
The extensive use of steel in the facade
has created high embodied energy in its
fabrication.

SCORES	
DENSITY & URBAN FORM	4
FLEXIBILITY & ADAPTABILITY	4
APPEARANCE & THRESHOLD	6
SPACE & LIGHT	12
CONSTRUCTION & SUSTAINABILITY	5
TOTAL	31

Right: Interior view from the 30th floor
Far right: 8 Spruce Street

5 **Warehouse Conversion:**
(a) Apartments
10 Spring Street, SoHo Renovated 1987

Many warehouses have been transformed into large studios and apartments because they make versatile spaces with their free plan, high ceilings and absence of loadbearing internal partitions. Number 10 Spring Street was originally an ammunitions factory and now accommodates four apartments. Jean-Luc has been living there with his family for 25 years.

SCORES	
DENSITY & URBAN FORM	15
FLEXIBILITY & ADAPTABILITY	13
APPEARANCE & THRESHOLD	16
SPACE & LIGHT	9
CONSTRUCTION & SUSTAINABILITY	3
TOTAL	56

Right: Typical Lower East Side: a factory made into flats
Far right: A unique interior

(b) Mixed Use
723 Washington Street,
Meatpacking District Renovated 2000

Ed owns Bennett Media studios, which he converted to house a gallery, studio/event space, a sound-recording studio and his penthouse apartment above. Large openings bring plentiful light into the sizeable spaces. These economically built industrial buildings are among the most flexible and sought-after homes in New York.

SCORES	
DENSITY & URBAN FORM	18
FLEXIBILITY & ADAPTABILITY	14
APPEARANCE & THRESHOLD	15
SPACE & LIGHT	18
CONSTRUCTION & SUSTAINABILITY	3
TOTAL	68

Right: Ed in his apartment above the studio spaces

6 **Suburban Development**
Levittown 1947

As the first and one of the largest mass-produced suburbs, Levittown quickly became a symbol of postwar US suburbia. Using precut timber increased speed and efficiency, and made for cost-effective construction. By July 1948, 30 houses were produced a day. The original construction format was a small house on one floor and an unfinished 'expansion attic' that could be completed and rented. Although Levittown is often thought of as homogeneous, the majority of houses have been comprehensively extended and personalised by their owners.

SCORES	
DENSITY & URBAN FORM	9
FLEXIBILITY & ADAPTABILITY	16
APPEARANCE & THRESHOLD	15
SPACE & LIGHT	11
CONSTRUCTION & SUSTAINABILITY	9
TOTAL	60

Levittown today

CHAPTER 13

PARIS

CITY STATISTICS

PARIS INTRA MUROS: 20 ARRONDISSEMENTS POPULATION	2,200,000
AVERAGE GROSS DENSITY, PEOPLE PER KM² (PER HA)	20,870/KM² (209/HA)
POPULATION GROWTH RATE PER ANNUM	0.45%
COST OF METRO TICKET FOR ONE STOP, € (LOCAL)	€1.70
AVERAGE EARNINGS PER ANNUM, € (LOCAL)	€19,000
AVERAGE HOUSE PRICE TO AVERAGE INCOME RATIO	17:1
AVERAGE NUMBER OF CARS PER 1,000 PEOPLE	460

Paris is an old-world city with a strong sense of culture that ensures its status as a major global capital. The 20 arrondissements that make up the urban core are collectively called the Intra Muros, literally 'between walls'. It is one of the densest inner urban cores of Europe, but as Parisians move from the expensive Intra Muros to the cheaper banlieue, (the outer ring of metropolitan suburbs), its population is shrinking.

From an original Celtic settlement colonised by the Romans, through centuries of walls torn down and rebuilt, a spiralling city has grown out from the Ile de la Cité.

In 1853 Napoleon III appointed Georges-Eugène Haussmann to rebuild Paris quickly, in order to reduce the high rate of unemployment and make the city 'revolution proof'. Haussmann created new roads and public monuments, installed sewers and built new apartment blocks that changed the architectural character of the city. Many of the medieval streets and homes were demolished and 15,000 people moved to the banlieue. The city was divided into districts with wide tree-lined boulevards and expansive gardens with geometric street layouts. Now a large ring road, the Périphérique, has replaced the ancient walls encircling the urban core.

The September 2005 riots that took place in the Grand Ensembles (large housing projects) in the banlieue highlighted social unrest and economic disparity between some pockets of the suburbs and the Intra Muros. In 2007, the French government revealed plans to invite 10 global architects to create 'the most sustainable post-Kyoto metropolis'.

Housing Typologies

The urban core of Paris has an architecturally coherent appearance, building heights are six storeys, and a majority of dwellings are Haussmann mixed-use or apartment buildings, with unified characteristics of tall windows and stone facades. The banlieue now has detached 'villa' houses and monolithic mid-rise and high-rise blocks, and a few housing blocks have appeared in the Intra Muros.

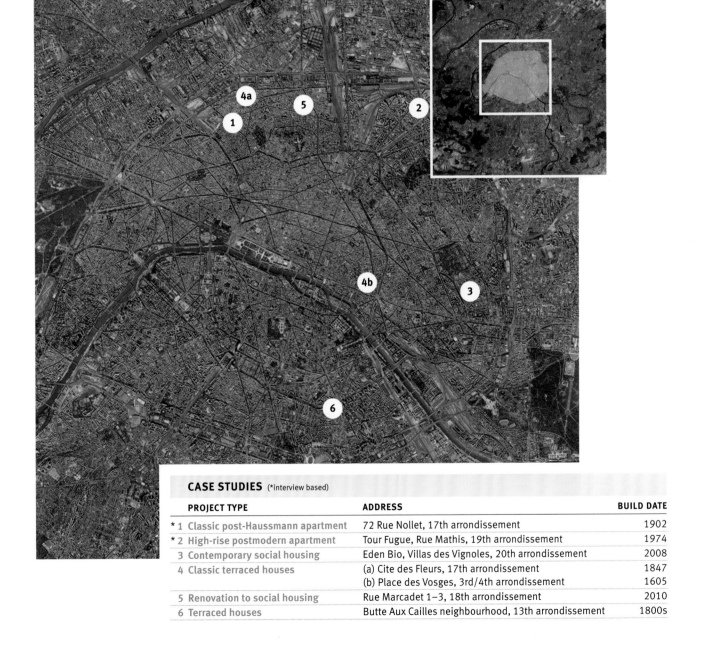

CASE STUDIES (*interview based)		
PROJECT TYPE	**ADDRESS**	**BUILD DATE**
* 1 Classic post-Haussmann apartment	72 Rue Nollet, 17th arrondissement	1902
* 2 High-rise postmodern apartment	Tour Fugue, Rue Mathis, 19th arrondissement	1974
3 Contemporary social housing	Eden Bio, Villas des Vignoles, 20th arrondissement	2008
4 Classic terraced houses	(a) Cite des Fleurs, 17th arrondissement	1847
	(b) Place des Vosges, 3rd/4th arrondissement	1605
5 Renovation to social housing	Rue Marcadet 1–3, 18th arrondissement	2010
6 Terraced houses	Butte Aux Cailles neighbourhood, 13th arrondissement	1800s

Christophe and Emilie

1 **Classic Post-Haussmann Apartment**
Residents: Emilie and Christophe
72 Rue Nollet, 17th arrondissement

Emilie, a photographers' agent, and her husband Christophe, a lawyer, bought their first-floor apartment in 2010. It is situated in the 17th arrondissement, which is a prime residential district in the west of Paris.

Density and urban form
Parisian apartments offer a high-quality way of living at a very high density. The terraced blocks were in fact built individually after the Haussmann period and were often designed by eminent architects. The maximum height of apartment buildings was limited to 20 metres, which through the use of generous ceiling heights resulted in buildings rarely exceeding six storeys. The internal courtyard offers light semi-private amenity space for residents and provides an entranceway to the rear apartments. The courtyard in Emilie's block is used for Fête des Voisines, meaning 'Neighbours' Party', a holiday introduced by the Parisian government.

Flexibility and adaptability
The apartment was originally designed in three distinct zones: social, private and service. But the rooms are generously proportioned and accessible from a common corridor, so they can be converted easily to accommodate different functions, as has been the case. Bedrooms for children and adults, and living space are distributed throughout the flat, and these arrangements have changed even during Emilie's time in the property. A service stairwell at the rear of the apartment would enable it to be divided into separate dwellings.

Dwelling Plan

Key:

A Entrance stairwell
B Entrance hall
C Living
D Bedroom
E Kitchen
F Service stairwell, closed
G Ensuite bathroom, previously bedroom
H Dining

0m   1   2   3   4   5

Appearance and threshold

Many Parisian apartment buildings situated on principal roads are mixed use at ground-floor level, ensuring a degree of vibrancy and urban efficiency. Rue Nollet, however, is predominantly residential. The block occupies the entire street frontage so that the principal living spaces look on to the street, giving a good visual connection. A large and ornate shared entrance opens directly from the pavement. This not only provides a sheltered and secure entrance for the main stair, which gives access to the front-facing flats such as Emilie's, but also connects through to the inner private courtyard, from which the rear flats are reached. Facades are regular, openings large, proportions well-composed.

Space and light

The six-storey surrounding blocks permit reasonable separation. With windows on all four elevations of the apartment, excellent light quality is achieved in each habitable space. Large windows punctuate the street-facing facade. This family lives on the bel-étage, the first floor, which is considered to be the most prestigious apartment in the building. Large windows from the rear rooms face on to the courtyard. A beautiful curved stained-glass bay window faces on to the courtyard from the dining room.

Construction and sustainability

The property is not insulated; however, thick masonry walls ensure good thermal mass and keep the spaces reasonably warm in winter. External shutters allow some noise control and provide solar shading during the hot summer months.

Cost and value

Situated in the affluent, predominantly residential 17th arrondissement of Paris, the cost to buy is extremely high at €8,500–10,000 per square metre: that is, up to 61 times the average salary. Post-Haussmann apartments are considered elegant, and very desirable. Parisian estate agents often refer to 'parquez, moulures et cheminée' or 'PMC' – original wood floors, cornicing and chimneys – as dwellings with such features demand a higher price than those without ●

SCORES	
DENSITY & URBAN FORM	19
FLEXIBILITY & ADAPTABILITY	12
APPEARANCE & THRESHOLD	16
SPACE & LIGHT	16
CONSTRUCTION & SUSTAINABILITY	2
TOTAL	**65**

CASE STUDY DATA	
Density (HR/ha):	1,200
Plot ratio:	3.12:1
Cost to buy:	€8,605/m²
Buy cost as a multiple of average earnings:	x 59
Floor area:	130m²
Plot area:	250m²
Outdoor private amenity space:	Shared courtyard
Floor-to-ceiling height:	3m
Floor area per habitable room:	14.5m²
Age of building (and style):	1902, neoclassical
Preferred room in the house:	Dining space, stained-glass room

Above left: The children's playroom

Above: The living room

Right: Rue Nollet

Right: Deirdre and Michael with their son

Below: View of the living room

2 **High-Rise Postmodern Apartment**
Residents: Deirdre and Michael
Tour Fugue, Rue Mathis, 19th arrondissement

Deirdre and Michael, both architects, live with their son in one of only a dozen Parisian high-rise blocks that were built during the early 1970s. These are not typical of the centre of Paris but they offer a cheaper alternative to the more prevalent Parisian apartment blocks.

Density and urban form
Tour Fugue is the tallest residential block in Paris. It is part of a competition-winning scheme, by Martin Van Treeck, of nearly 2,000 dwellings on 2.4 hectares using 'organ pipe' tower forms and sculpted tiered low-rise blocks. Shared services for the residents include a 25m swimming pool, doctor's surgery, nursery and launderette. The high density ensures that the services are well used.

Flexibility and adaptability
Originally a one-bed apartment, it had enough slack spaces – corridors, large cupboards and a dressing room – that the internal layout could be reconfigured to accommodate two bedrooms and a large living area. The open-plan living room is altered throughout the day to office, dining room, play space and projector room. Short of buying an adjoining flat, the property cannot be extended.

Space and light
The scheme pays attention to light quality and internal living conditions. Each apartment has an outward-looking aspect on to the city. The large glazed doors provide abundant daylight into the living room, and the ceiling height makes the space feel larger. The view over the city was the deciding factor in buying the flat: 'it would be a different matter if the flat were on the lower floors – we'd have no view and less light, and the place would seem claustrophobic'.

Appearance and threshold
The planned spaces immediately surrounding the high-density blocks are unsuccessful. The complex shuts out urban street life, and the overshadowed, empty, large landscaped areas occupied by gangs make the entranceways to Tour Fugue feel unsafe at night.

Construction and sustainability
The block is constructed from reinforced concrete with no insulation and single-glazed windows. Sustainability was not high on the agenda in the 1970s. The tower houses the circulation and services within a triangular core. With utility bills shared between the block – €250 per month during the summer and €350 during the winter – there is little financial incentive to be sparing or sustainable.

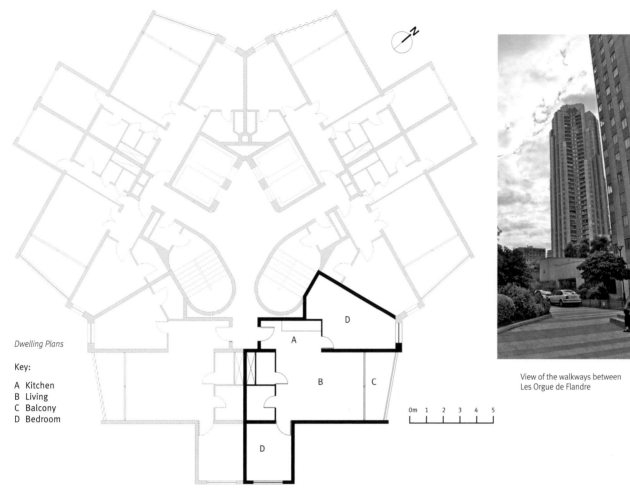

Dwelling Plans

Key:

A Kitchen
B Living
C Balcony
D Bedroom

View of the walkways between
Les Orgue de Flandre

Cost and value

The north-eastern 19th district is the cheapest and densest area of
Paris, and the only place left in the Intra Muros that young middle-
income professionals can afford to buy. In line with Parisian property
prices, the apartment has increased in value from €220,000 to
€400,000 in five years ●

SCORES

DENSITY & URBAN FORM	4
FLEXIBILITY & ADAPTABILITY	9
APPEARANCE & THRESHOLD	1
SPACE & LIGHT	15
CONSTRUCTION & SUSTAINABILITY	3
TOTAL	32

CASE STUDY DATA

Density (HR/ha):	558
Plot ratio:	1.5:1
Cost to buy:	€7,142/m²
Buy cost as a multiple of average earnings:	x 21
Floor area:	56m²
Plot area:	10,000m²
Outdoor private amenity space:	3m² balcony
Floor-to-ceiling height:	2.5m
Floor area per habitable room:	15m²
Age of building (and style):	1974, postmodern Brutalist
Preferred room in the house:	Flexible living space

3 Contemporary Social Housing
Eden Bio, Villas des Vignoles,
20th arrondissement 2008

This social housing development, designed by architect Edouard François, includes 100 social apartments and studios, community rooms and a small restaurant. Consultation with residents resulted in two simple blocks that appear as collections of individual houses, with cladding differentiating the bays. The scheme is four storeys high and punctuated with pitched roofs, front gardens and south-facing balconies. Red shingles wrap each of the roofs and flank-wall surfaces, and open timber staircases and vertical gardens overlook an internal street just 2 metres wide. This is an excellent high-density urban development, creating a sense of belonging and community.

SCORES	
DENSITY & URBAN FORM	19
FLEXIBILITY & ADAPTABILITY	11
APPEARANCE & THRESHOLD	18
SPACE & LIGHT	10
CONSTRUCTION & SUSTAINABILITY	7
TOTAL	65

The central semi-private street in Eden Bio

4 Classic Terraced Houses

(a) Cité des Fleurs,
17th arrondissement 1847

Cité des Fleurs consists of two rows of terraced houses divided by a 230-metre-long communal passageway. This typology is unique to the urban layout of Paris but exemplifies a diverse mix of family homes and apartments within a terraced form. While equal-sized plots were sold to individuals to develop within strict design codes, the appearance of each property is personally styled and typically elaborate.

(b) Place des Vosges,
3rd/4th arrondissement 1605

Described as one of Europe's most beautiful squares, Place des Vosges is the oldest planned square in Paris, 140 metres by 140 metres, with four-storey private courtyard buildings. The facade is composed of tall French windows and a brick-and-stone facade in elegant proportions. High density, low rise, flexible and adaptable, mixed-use areas such as these are the gems of Paris.

SCORES	
DENSITY & URBAN FORM	19
FLEXIBILITY & ADAPTABILITY	13
APPEARANCE & THRESHOLD	18
SPACE & LIGHT	20
CONSTRUCTION & SUSTAINABILITY	2
TOTAL	72

Above: Cité des Fleurs
Below: Place des Vosges

Rue Marcadet

5 Renovation to Social Housing
Rue Marcadet 1–3,
18th arrondissement 2010

Seventy apartments form an urban perimeter fronting the street and securing the inner courtyard for residents. The building has been upgraded for sustainability, with thermal insulation and solar panels on the roofs. The facades are animated with small and large window openings and balconies staggered in a random pattern, and bright yellow external shutters provide privacy. The blocks have been configured as flats accessed from shared open staircases, when terraces could have been built at the same density.

SCORES	
DENSITY & URBAN FORM	15
FLEXIBILITY & ADAPTABILITY	10
APPEARANCE & THRESHOLD	8
SPACE & LIGHT	10
CONSTRUCTION & SUSTAINABILITY	11
TOTAL	54

6 Terraced Houses
Butte Aux Cailles neighbourhood, 13th arrondissement 1800s

Within the narrow, cobbled streets sit these individually decorated town houses. They are charming and perfectly scaled urban dwellings. A majority of houses were built in terraces with front and rear gardens. The shared party walls enabled a very flexible form with cost-effective construction.

SCORES	
DENSITY & URBAN FORM	19
FLEXIBILITY & ADAPTABILITY	13
APPEARANCE & THRESHOLD	18
SPACE & LIGHT	19
CONSTRUCTION & SUSTAINABILITY	3
TOTAL	72

Right: Narrow, cobbled lanes create intimate spaces
Far right: Houses in Butte Aux Cailles

CHAPTER 14

BERLIN

CITY STATISTICS

BERLIN: 12 BEZIRKE POPULATION	3,500,000
AVERAGE GROSS DENSITY, PEOPLE PER KM² (PER HA)	3,900/KM² (39/HA)
POPULATION GROWTH RATE PER ANNUM	0.3%
COST OF METRO TICKET FOR ONE STOP, € (LOCAL)	€1.40
AVERAGE EARNINGS PER ANNUM, € (LOCAL)	€27,500
AVERAGE HOUSE PRICE TO AVERAGE INCOME RATIO	6:1
AVERAGE NUMBER OF CARS PER 1,000 PEOPLE	319

Described by Berlin's mayor in 2004, Klaus Wowereit, as 'poor but sexy', Berlin is gaining a reputation as a city of knowledge and culture, and while it is not the strongest of cities economically and is suffering from population decline, it offers a high quality of life for relatively little cost.

In 1862, James Hobrecht, chief city planner, drew up Berlin's expansion development plan to create a utopian and socially mixed urban environment. It set out a wide-mesh system of avenues and building lines, but did not designate building functions or public spaces.

Berlin's building stock significantly diminished during the second world war. The Berlin Wall divided East and West Berlin for 28 years, from 1961 to 1989. During that time, West Berlin's economy grew and its standard of living improved, while East Berlin's property and industry were nationalised. Nevertheless, subsequent merciless planning policies in both the East and the West resulted in the demolition of the majority of Berlin. Between 1940 and 2010, approximately 60% of the city was rebuilt.

The Internationale Bauausstellung Berlin (IBA), literally 'international building exhibition', consisted of a number of exemplary redevelopment projects in West Berlin, described as 'The Inner City as Residential Area'. Initiated in 1979 and completed in 1987, it was an ambitious attempt to 're-marry architecture and the city'. It commissioned high-profile architects to integrate new buildings – housing, schools and public spaces – into the urban fabric, running in a band east to west across the centre of the city.

Housing Typologies

Berlin is now home to diverse creative communities. Ownership rates are lower than in the rest of Germany, at 13%. Approximately 10% of the population lives in single- or two-family buildings, the remainder living in older multi-family blocks (known as Altbau) or linear concrete constructions (known as Plattenbau).

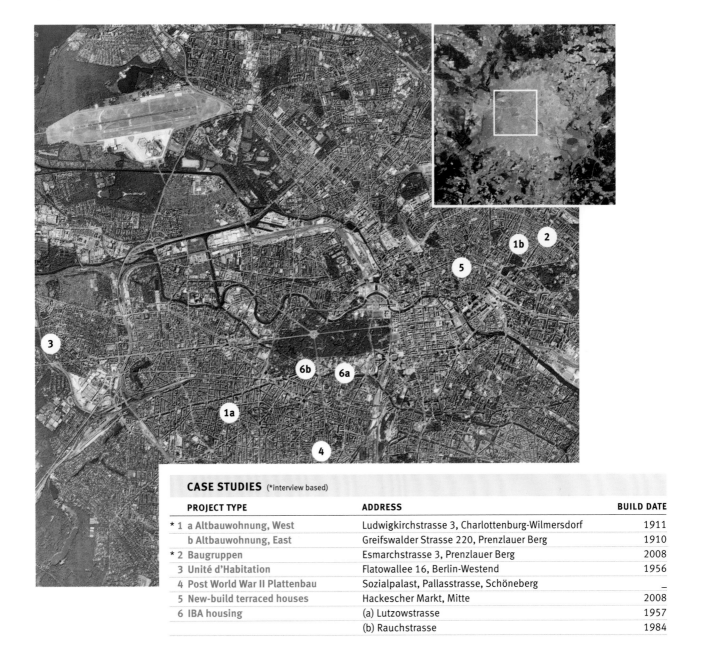

CASE STUDIES (*interview based)

	PROJECT TYPE	ADDRESS	BUILD DATE
* 1	a Altbauwohnung, West	Ludwigkirchstrasse 3, Charlottenburg-Wilmersdorf	1911
	b Altbauwohnung, East	Greifswalder Strasse 220, Prenzlauer Berg	1910
* 2	Baugruppen	Esmarchstrasse 3, Prenzlauer Berg	2008
3	Unité d'Habitation	Flatowallee 16, Berlin-Westend	1956
4	Post World War II Plattenbau	Sozialpalast, Pallasstrasse, Schöneberg	–
5	New-build terraced houses	Hackescher Markt, Mitte	2008
6	IBA housing	(a) Lutzowstrasse	1957
		(b) Rauchstrasse	1984

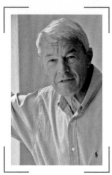

1 (a) **Altbauwohnung, West**

Resident: Christof Helberger
Ludwigkirchstrasse 3, Charlottenburg-Wilmersdorf

Altbau properties constructed between 1880 and 1920 are generally divided into apartments, Christof Helberger lives with his wife in an Altbau apartment in Ludwigkirchstrasse, West Berlin.

Density and urban form
Christof's front apartment, a Vorderhaus, literally 'front house', faces onto a wide tree-lined street with small shops on the ground floor. The block plan is a C-shape, formed around a central internal courtyard; the larger more expensive flats face the street, and the courtyard provides semi-private open space, views and natural light, as well as access to the rear apartments.

Flexibility and adaptability
Most large Altbau apartments contain a classic Berlinerzimmer, a large flexible room acting as a connection between the front and rear of the apartment, which removes the need for a corridor. The deep, narrow plan creates a clear modular layout for the rooms. Christof has used the rear stairwell from the courtyard to create an independent access to his office. This arrangement also gives the potential to subdivide the flat into two lettings.

Above: Christof Helberger

Right: The Altbau: Ludwigkirchstrasse

Far right: View of the shared internal courtyard

Dwelling Plans

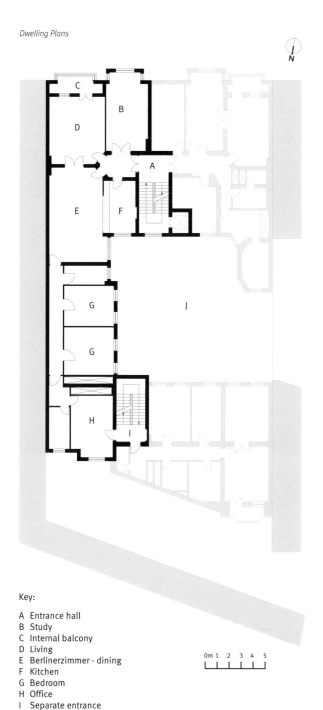

Key:

A   Entrance hall
B   Study
C   Internal balcony
D   Living
E   Berlinerzimmer - dining
F   Kitchen
G   Bedroom
H   Office
I   Separate entrance
J   Shared internal courtyard

0m 1 2 3 4 5

Appearance and threshold

The Altbau elevation is based on classical proportions with vertical windows punctuating the painted masonry facades. A large central sheltered entrance to the apartments is accessed from the street and leads to a generous semi-private stairwell giving access to the larger front-facing apartments. Smaller rear apartments are accessed through the semi-private courtyard.

Space and light

Christof's apartment has large rooms, high ceilings and a private balcony. A single window in the corner of the finely detailed Berlinerzimmer provides daylight and views over the courtyard, and generous proportions evoke a sense of openness, charm and elegance: in his words, a space 'with dignity'.

CASE STUDY DATA

Density (HR/ha):	903
Plot ratio:	3:1
Cost to buy:	€4,450/m²
Cost to rent:	€14/m²/m
Buy cost as a multiple of average earnings:	x 31
Floor area:	191m²
Plot area:	830m²
Outdoor private amenity space:	5m² loggia and shared courtyard
Floor-to-ceiling height:	4m
Floor area per habitable room:	23m²
Age of building (and style):	1911, 'Altbau'
Preferred room in the house:	'Berlinerzimmer' living room

Construction and sustainability

Altbau were constructed using traditional building techniques and materials, masonry walls and timber beams. This building is maintained by a tenants' management group, and Christof's annual energy cost is €500.

Cost and value

Under the Town Planning Act of 1875, property owners were required to pay for a half-share of the street corresponding to the length of frontage, and this led to blocks being constructed narrowly and deeply with back buildings. Hobrecht's Plan was heavily criticised during the industrial period but his vision is now appreciated, the difference in size between the front and rear apartments encouraging a greater social mix.

The same building form was found in many other parts of the city, including the deprived and eroded districts of East Berlin. The following is a typical example.

SCORES	
DENSITY & URBAN FORM	18
FLEXIBILITY & ADAPTABILITY	14
APPEARANCE & THRESHOLD	18
SPACE & LIGHT	16
CONSTRUCTION & SUSTAINABILITY	3
TOTAL	**69**

View through the Berlinerzimmer

1 (b) **Altbauwohnung, East**

Residents: Jutta and Friedrich
Greifswalder Strasse 220, Prenzlauer Berg

Jutta lives in an unrenovated Altbau situated in East Berlin. The facade and external areas are in a poor state of repair and the property appears to be derelict. Just 10 to 15 years ago this former working-class district was run down and neglected by the municipality but cherished by its young community as an 'underground' creative hub. Now the area is full of boutiques, organic shops and busy restaurants. Jutta used to share this Altbau with three friends but now lives here with her partner and baby daughter. The Berlinerzimmer is also a key part of the apartment for Jutta, offering a large flexible open space which was previously used as an entertainment space but is now a sleep and play space for the baby ●

Top: Interior view of Altbauwohunung East   *Above:* Exterior view of Altbauwohnung East

Left: Carsten at his front door

2 **Baugruppen**

Residents: Carsten and Ulrike
Esmarchstrasse 3, Prenzlauer Berg

Individuals and families pool their resources to form Baugruppen, or housing cooperatives to fund construction and commission designs to develop new homes. This gives greater control over architectural and built quality, the costs and the administration of their properties.

The phenomenon of Baugruppen in Berlin is a defiant, popular and innovative response to traditional property development. Carsten Probst, a writer, and his wife Ulrike Draesuen, an art critic, live on the fourth floor of Stadthaus e3, an award-winning Baugruppe project completed in 2008. They came across the Baugruppe by chance; on a flyer attached to a lamp-post in a nearby park. The three originators decided that it was the best place to find like-minded people to build a seven-storey wooden town house, with an emphasis on sustainability and cost-effectiveness.

Density and Urban Form
Located in an urban infill site in the city centre, the mixed-use block integrates very well in the streetscape. The ground-floor premises are occupied by the Baugruppe architect, Kaden + Klingbeil. Each apartment is accessed via an external staircase, connected to the block by concrete walkways.

Dwelling Plan

Key:

A Separate open stair core
B Balcony entrance
C Entrance hall
D Bedroom
E Balcony
F Study
G Kitchen/dining
H Living

0m 1 2 3 4 5

Flexibility and adaptability

Two concrete cores run the entire height of the building for structural stability and services distribution, with clear-span floor layouts subdivided and arranged as desired. The resultant floor plates are loft-like spaces, accommodating a variety of family apartments and small work studios.

Appearance and threshold

The timber-frame construction is finished in white render so that it complements the surrounding existing painted stone and render facades, but with a clean and modern finish. The openings and balconies are in an attractive 'chessboard' configuration. The spacious loggias in front of the apartment doors are for communal use by all the building's residents.

Space and light

Each apartment receives light from three elevations through full-height vertical-format windows. Light is able to penetrate into the deep plan through translucent panels in the partition walls.

Construction and sustainability

Since the Baugruppe is made up of the end-users, there is genuine collaborative drive for high-quality sustainable and cost-effective methods of construction. The building consists of in-situ concrete slabs, constructed one floor per week. Laminated timber columns with steel connections were craned in once each floor slab was poured. The freestanding open concrete staircase is an escape route that can neither burn nor fill with smoke.

Cost and value

Sound architectural design, use of space and careful detailing have yielded a property whose perceived value is high compared to build costs. The gross square-metre cost of €1,900–2,400, is approximately 25% lower than normal developer-led projects in Berlin. This initiative was supported with funding from Berlin's local government, and it challenges traditional notions of property development ●

SCORES

DENSITY & URBAN FORM	17
FLEXIBILITY & ADAPTABILITY	17
APPEARANCE & THRESHOLD	18
SPACE & LIGHT	17
CONSTRUCTION & SUSTAINABILITY	14
TOTAL	83

Above right: Interior view

Above far right: Exterior view

Right: Esmarchstrasse

CASE STUDY DATA

Density (HR/ha):	583
Plot ratio:	2.64:1
Cost to buy:	€1,040/m² (build cost)
Buy cost as a multiple of average earnings:	x 7.7
Floor area:	204m²
Plot area:	540m²
Outdoor private amenity space:	10m² balcony and shared garden
Floor-to-ceiling height:	2.6m
Floor area per habitable room:	19m²
Age of building (and style):	2008, contemporary sustainable
Preferred room in the house:	Flexible living space

3 Unité d'Habitation
Flatowallee 16, Berlin-Westend 1956

Completed in 1956, this linear block was designed as a small city with spacious duplex apartments accommodating different housing types, from single dwellings to family residences. Using the Unité d'Habitation concept developed by Le Corbusier, the building comprises 530 apartments over 17 levels, accessed through 'internal streets' or wide corridors, where residents can enjoy social interaction. Each house has a private balcony, forming a grid expressed on the facade; this allows indirect light to enter, reducing excessive solar radiation. The building, supported on columns for parking spaces, is set in a garden, and the entire complex is detached from the surrounding urban infrastructure. It originally incorporated public facilities, such as shops and a children's nursery, which no longer function.

Unité d'Habitation view of the exterior

SCORES

DENSITY & URBAN FORM	3
FLEXIBILITY & ADAPTABILITY	6
APPEARANCE & THRESHOLD	7
SPACE & LIGHT	12
CONSTRUCTION & SUSTAINABILITY	4
TOTAL	32

4 Post WWII Plattenbau
East and West Berlin

Plattenbau were created to provide economic family housing, after the second world war. By using standardised pre-fabricated concrete to make estates in simple four-storey blocks, the government could house families quickly in areas of the city centre that had been badly war-damaged. These estates were characterised by functional monotony and poorly articulated external spaces, but many of the 300,000 Plattenbau homes have been renovated with colourful facades, balconies and updated building entrances.

SCORES

DENSITY & URBAN FORM	7
FLEXIBILITY & ADAPTABILITY	8
APPEARANCE & THRESHOLD	6
SPACE & LIGHT	9
CONSTRUCTION & SUSTAINABILITY	0
TOTAL	30

Typical Plattenbau housing in Pallasstrasse, Schoneberg

5 **New-build Terraced Houses**
Hackescher Markt, Mitte 2008

This new terrace of tall, narrow town houses sits opposite the monolithic modernist facade of a government building and is an attempt to bring new ownership into the area. The properties are all configured on narrow but deep plots, with different heights, facades and construction materials for each building. Because of high site value and bespoke design, some Berliners regard them as elitist. They display the characteristic of Amsterdam's Borneo project (Chapter 3), providing instant diversity but without longer-term flexibility.

New-build terrace houses, Kurstrasse, Hackescher Markt

SCORES	
DENSITY & URBAN FORM	19
FLEXIBILITY & ADAPTABILITY	9
APPEARANCE & THRESHOLD	13
SPACE & LIGHT	16
CONSTRUCTION & SUSTAINABILITY	1
TOTAL	58

6 **Interbau 1957 and IBA 1984**

Berlin's International Building Exhibitions (1957 and 1984) celebrated rebuilding programmes, particularly in the field of housing. In the 1957 exhibition, contributions from internationally renowned architects including Aalto, Gropius, Jacobson and Neimeyer created 'Housing in the City of Tomorrow', enhancing West Berlin's new urban image. The results were apartment blocks representing their respective approaches to mass housing. These mid-height blocks are set within landscaped grounds, with large atrium entrances to the generous apartments.

Above: IBA Townhouses, Lutzowstrasse
Below: IBA Apartments, Rauchstrasse

(a) IBA Lutzowstrasse, West Berlin
(b) IBA Rauchstrasse, West Berlin

The Case Studies are taken from the IBA 1984 (International Bauausstellung) which promoted 'The Inner City as Residential Area'; but what was considered contemporary urbanism then, now looks rather dated. However, the mid-density infrastructure of public and private spaces has left a positive and affordable legacy for Berlin's inhabitants.

SCORES	
DENSITY & URBAN FORM	16
FLEXIBILITY & ADAPTABILITY	10
APPEARANCE & THRESHOLD	11
SPACE & LIGHT	11
CONSTRUCTION & SUSTAINABILITY	2
TOTAL	50

CHAPTER 15

MEXICO CITY

CITY STATISTICS

MEXICO CITY: 16 DELAGACIONES POPULATION	8,850,000
AVERAGE GROSS DENSITY, PEOPLE PER KM^2 (PER HA)	5,960/KM^2 (60/HA)
POPULATION GROWTH RATE PER ANNUM	2%
COST OF METRO TICKET FOR ONE STOP, € (LOCAL)	€0.20 (MEX$3)
AVERAGE EARNINGS PER ANNUM, € (LOCAL)	€15,800 (MEX$263,000)
AVERAGE HOUSE PRICE TO AVERAGE INCOME RATIO	14:1
AVERAGE NUMBER OF CARS PER 1,000 PEOPLE	460

Since the 1970s, Mexico City has become notorious for its phenomenal rate of population growth and extreme social and urban polarisation. This can be witnessed on the outskirts of the city, where the telecom billionaire Carlos Slim's luxury high-rises overlook sprawling self-built slums.

The Aztecs originally built the city in 1325, and in 1521 the Spanish rebuilt it in accordance with European urban standards, incorporating important Aztec buildings and avenues. From the 1900s its population doubled in size every 10 years, and government policies supporting road construction led to unregulated urban sprawl. The built-up area expanded from 23 to 154,710 square kilometres between 1900 and 2000.

In 1985, following a magnitude 8.0 earthquake that killed an estimated 35,000 people, new building regulations were put into place, opening up spaces in the urban fabric and shifting patterns of growth and density. Fear of increasing crime in the historic city centre has led to the creation of suburban, gated communities up to several hours' journey from the metropolis, and commuter traffic causes severe air pollution. In 2000, the Federal District (FD) government introduced policy guidelines, Bandos Dos, in order to repopulate the city centre and restrict urban sprawl.

Housing Typologies

Today the city has thriving architectural initiatives, driven by inspired young architects working in tandem with the government, to provide new high-density housing in the city centre. Sprawling low-density housing accommodates more than 60% of Mexico City's population. 'Colonias Populares' are irregular settlements of self-built and mainly owner-occupied dwellings, and 10% of all housing consists of classic vecindad mixed-use housing types. Vecindades were built as multi-family tenements to rent to low-income artisans, but their popularity resulted in the creation of different styles and generosities – ranging from low-income dwellings to architect-designed clusters. The rows of new-build concrete houses built on the peripheries of Mexico City from the 1940s, also ambiguously termed vecindades, are loosely based on the classic vecindad urban form, but fail to deliver the high-quality urban infrastructure created by high urban density, local facilities and access to public transport.

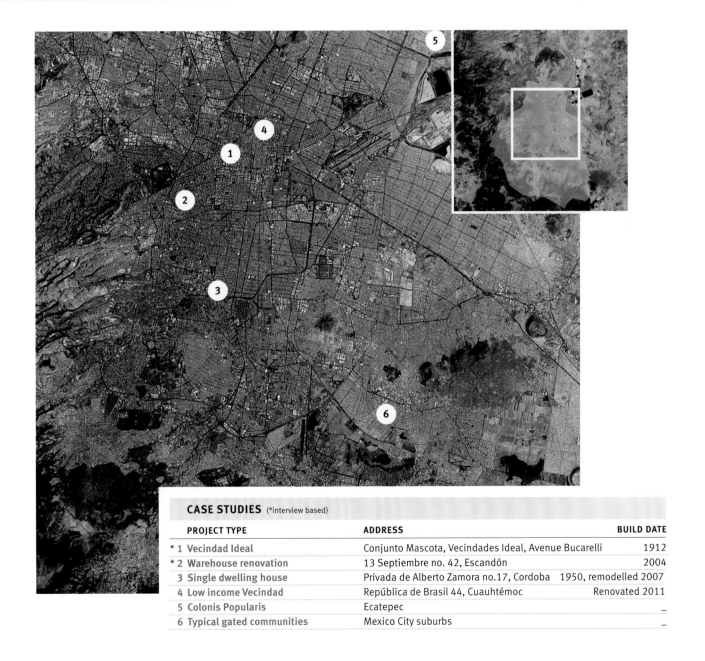

CASE STUDIES (*interview based)

	PROJECT TYPE	ADDRESS	BUILD DATE
* 1	Vecindad Ideal	Conjunto Mascota, Vecindades Ideal, Avenue Bucarelli	1912
* 2	Warehouse renovation	13 Septiembre no. 42, Escandón	2004
3	Single dwelling house	Privada de Alberto Zamora no.17, Cordoba	1950, remodelled 2007
4	Low income Vecindad	República de Brasil 44, Cuauhtémoc	Renovated 2011
5	Colonis Popularis	Ecatepec	–
6	Typical gated communities	Mexico City suburbs	–

1 **Vecindad Ideal**

Residents: Mariana and Abraham
Conjunto Mascota, Vecindades Ideal, Avenue Bucarelli

Mariana and Abraham live in a classic vecindad, Calle Ideal, literally 'Ideal Street'. It is part of a scheme containing 176 apartments in three adjoining internal streets. Originally built for cigarette factory workers, its inhabitants abandoned Calle Ideal during the 1980s as the area was suffering from increasing levels of crime. Today the government is pushing to redevelop inner-city infrastructure, and young professionals are moving back to these districts. Mariana and Abraham bought and renovated their apartment in 2010.

Density and urban form

The vecindad consists of two-storey terraced blocks with well-composed facade details configured around a beautiful but simple landscaped patio. The dwellings are configured back-to-back and are provided with light wells and courtyards to introduce natural light into the inner rooms. This arrangement results in a very compact overall geometry yielding very high density for a building complex of modest height. All the dwellings are apartments distributed over the ground and first floors, with basement facilities for laundry and storage. The shape of the block directly responds to the grid structure of the city, and a sense of community is born out of daily interaction facilitated by the semi-private courtyard.

Dwelling Plan

Key:

A Private stair from ground level
B Study
C Living
D Dining
E Kitchen
F Bedroom

Above left: Calle Ideal

Above right: Mariana and Abraham with their son

0m 1 2 3 4 5

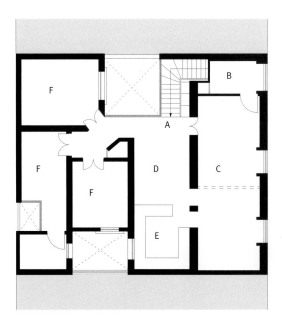

Flexibility and adaptability

The architecture, materials and historical sense of permanence give it a glorious haptic sensibility, and the well-maintained gardens evoke a sense of 'home'. Ground-floor units or 'accesorias', are businesses situated within the corner frontage of the block, and appear in most inner-city vecindades. Owners are usually inhabitants of the vecindad, and the activities within them vary from convenience stores to small offices.

Appearance and threshold

Its residents use the shared patio garden throughout the year as an internal street, and this gives welcome separation from the busy adjacent thoroughfare and provides security.

Mariana and Abraham did not want to lose the historically important features of the vecindad, so they have renovated the original features – the patio doors, cornicing, windows – while complementing the space with modern fixtures and furniture.

Space and light

A private internal light well to the rear of their dwelling ensures that light can flood into every room in the property. The exceptionally generous ceilings make the relatively small floor plan feel generous, open and very bright.

Construction and sustainability

The construction is concrete and brick, with stone openings. The floors and roof are made from wooden beams. The fact that the stone detailing and brick walls are still intact following the earthquake of 1985 is testament to the sound construction of this particular building. Very little work had to be done to the structure, and Mariana and Abraham opened up the interior walls so that 'the spaces would flow into one another'.

Cost and value

Mariana and Abraham Gonzales bought their property for MEX $1.5m (€90,670), and spent about MEX $50,000 (€3,000) on the renovation of the property ●

Above left: View of the internal light well

Above right: The middle income vecindades have large bright rooms

CASE STUDY DATA

Density (HR/ha):	612
Plot ratio:	1.3:1
Cost to buy:	€715/m² (Mex$11,900/m²)
Buy cost as a multiple of average earnings:	x 5.7
Floor area:	130m²
Plot area:	196m²
Outdoor private amenity space:	Shared internal garden street
Floor-to-ceiling height:	3.7m
Floor area per habitable room:	14m²
Age of building (and style):	1912, classic courtyard house
Preferred room in the house:	Living room

SCORES

DENSITY & URBAN FORM	20
FLEXIBILITY & ADAPTABILITY	16
APPEARANCE & THRESHOLD	19
SPACE & LIGHT	18
CONSTRUCTION & SUSTAINABILITY	3
TOTAL	**76**

2 **Warehouse Renovation**
Residents: Sofia and Jorge
13 Septiembre no. 42, Escandón

The architects, JSa, preserved the exterior of this 1950s' warehouse and placed 37 two-story loft residences inside the perimeter of the structure. Sofia and Jorge enjoy living in their neighbourhood and the loft apartment. They rent the property, and would like to buy a place of their own when they start a family.

Density and urban form
The project is a sustainable use of urban fabric as the architects created a design that allowed its partial preservation. They placed the homes inside the perimeter of the structure, an arrangement that kept the warehouse's distinctive windows and much of its overall exterior. All the building's core elements were removed, however, to create a central communal courtyard space.

Flexibility and adaptability
The original warehouse plan, with clear structural spans and large windows, presents a very versatile and adaptable structure to convert for a multiplicity of uses. The lofts are configured so that some families are able to combine two loft spaces, if available, to create an enlarged dwelling space.

Appearance and threshold
The central courtyard is intended to evoke the vecindad form. With a central stairwell and gantries five metres apart, it was conceived as a flexible communal area. However, the space is dominated by access structures, and the aluminium cladding and concrete combination makes the area inhospitable, so it never performs the intended communal function.

Space and light
The existing windows and combined double-height spaces and mezzanine levels provide compact yet generous-feeling apartments. Sofia and Jorge's apartment has two habitable rooms within 54m². The kitchen and bathrooms are designed to maximise storage and habitable floor space.

Each apartment has either a garden space or roof terrace, and this characteristic was the main draw for Sofia and Jorge.

Above centre: Exterior view of 13 de Septiembre

Far left: Double-height space at the front of the apartment

Left: Sofia and Jorge at their front door

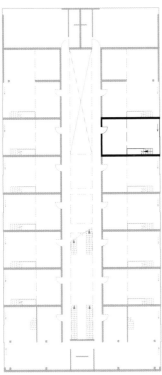

Block plan 1:500

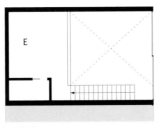

E

Level 02

N

Dwelling Plans

Key:

A Entrance
B Study/dining
C Living
D Garden
E Bedroom
F Kitchen

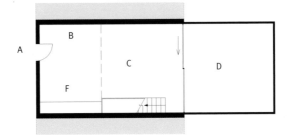

A

B

C

D

F

Level 01

0m 1 2 3 4 5

SCORES	
DENSITY & URBAN FORM	9
FLEXIBILITY & ADAPTABILITY	13
APPEARANCE & THRESHOLD	15
SPACE & LIGHT	10
CONSTRUCTION & SUSTAINABILITY	10
TOTAL	**57**

Construction and sustainability

The building's finishes express its essentially industrial character. Retaining the existing building envelope, there is no need for construction of foundations and external structure; therefore less building material and embodied energy are used. The temperate climate in Mexico City does not require double glazing, and therefore the existing windows to the front facade were retained.

Cost and value

Bandos Dos and renovation projects changed Escandón from a lower-middle-class district to a mixed-income neighbourhood. The cost to convert the warehouse was 30% less than the typical cost of constructing a new-build housing scheme, yet these apartments are worth three times more than surrounding dwellings. This project is a prime example of sensitive well-designed spaces notably increasing the perceived value of a property and neighbourhood. The smart use of space, increased density of the street and the area, local amenities and good transport links to the city centre are all contributing factors ●

CASE STUDY DATA	
Density (HR/ha):	653
Plot ratio:	1.7:1
Cost to buy:	€1,695/m² (Mex$28,000/m²)
Cost to rent/m²/m	€12.50/m²/m (Mex$204/m²/m)
Buy cost as a multiple of average earnings:	x 5.7
Floor area:	54m²
Plot area:	1,700m2
Outdoor private amenity space:	20m² terrace
Floor-to-ceiling height:	2.6m, living room 5.2m
Floor area per habitable room:	19m²
Age of building (and style):	2004, contemporary
Preferred room in the house:	Double-height living space

3 **Single Dwelling House**
Privada de Alberto Zamora no.17,
Cordoba 1950, remodelled 2007

A beautifully detailed detached house with
roof terrace, hidden behind a living garden
wall, was completely renovated in 2007,
integrating large windows and skylights
to create generous open space. The entire
house looks inwards towards a private
garden, which is typical of the area but to
the detriment of street life. This urban form
contributes to the perception of unsafe
streets. Large open-plan rooms and a lack
of hierarchy on the ground floor give spatial
flexibility.

Architect-designed house in Cordoba
Right: Open plan living room

SCORES	
DENSITY & URBAN FORM	10
FLEXIBILITY & ADAPTABILITY	10
APPEARANCE & THRESHOLD	14
SPACE & LIGHT	17
CONSTRUCTION & SUSTAINABILITY	2
TOTAL	53

4 **Vecindad Low Income**
República de Brasil 44, Cuauhtémoc
Renovated 2011

The vecindad form is recognised by the FD
government as an integral contribution to
the metropolis. This renovation, by JSa, of a
low-income vecindad in the Federal District
is part of the housing renewal programme,
and it is occupied by five low-income
families and a wedding-gown shop. The
symmetry of the inner courtyard is a major
architectural element, and the central open
space is essential to the function of the
dwelling. It is infused with the physical
and social structure of the city and gives a
strong sense of community by providing an
integral link between the vecindad and the
daily street activities .

Courtyard to low income vecindades
Right: Modest, bright yellow front elevation

SCORES	
DENSITY & URBAN FORM	19
FLEXIBILITY & ADAPTABILITY	12
APPEARANCE & THRESHOLD	18
SPACE & LIGHT	6
CONSTRUCTION & SUSTAINABILITY	6
TOTAL	61

5 Colonis Popularis
Ecatepec

Colonias Populares cover approximately half of the urbanised area and house more than 60% of the population. Irregular settlements, unauthorised land development and construction, and poor urban service infrastructure are typical. However, second-generation inhabitants are improving the fabric of these fragile constructions and creating more permanent communities.

SCORES	
DENSITY & URBAN FORM	14
FLEXIBILITY & ADAPTABILITY	8
APPEARANCE & THRESHOLD	4
SPACE & LIGHT	0
CONSTRUCTION & SUSTAINABILITY	3
TOTAL	29

Colonis Popularis

Suburban gated communities

6 Typical Gated Communities
Mexico City suburbs

Homogeneous low-density gated communities extend the urban sprawl up to 40 kilometres from the city centre, leading to insufferably long daily commutes for most residents and severe pollution. Small interior spaces and unsustainable concrete construction create poor architectural and urban quality, and the deserted streets and gated lanes display little communal or commercial activity.

SCORES	
DENSITY & URBAN FORM	9
FLEXIBILITY & ADAPTABILITY	3
APPEARANCE & THRESHOLD	10
SPACE & LIGHT	6
CONSTRUCTION & SUSTAINABILITY	1
TOTAL	29

CHAPTER 16

SHANGHAI

CITY STATISTICS

SHANGHAI MUNICIPALITY: 18 DISTRICTS POPULATION	23,000,000
AVERAGE GROSS DENSITY, PEOPLE PER KM² (PER HA)	3,630/KM² (36/HA)
POPULATION GROWTH RATE PER ANNUM	3.4%
COST OF METRO TICKET FOR ONE STOP, € (LOCAL)	€0.40 (3 CNY)
AVERAGE EARNINGS PER ANNUM, € (LOCAL)	€6,000 (46,760 CNY)
AVERAGE HOUSE PRICE TO AVERAGE INCOME RATIO	30
AVERAGE NUMBER OF CARS PER 1,000 PEOPLE	140

One of the world's most thriving and cosmopolitan cities, Shanghai funds over 12% of government revenues and handles more than 25% of trade passing through China's ports. Its metropolitan population in 2010 was 23m and driven by inward migration.

On a piece of land of only 2.04 square kilometres, Shanghai's location at the mouth of the Yangtze led to its development as a superior port open to foreign trade. The British established a concession under the treaty of Nanking in 1842, with the French, Americans and Japanese establishing strategic territories bordering the Huangpu river. These concession districts held complete administrative autonomy, and separate planning strategies led to an organic pattern of street networks, an inconsistent street grid and urban blocks varying in size and shape.

During the 1930s, Shanghai prospered as a centre of commerce between east and west. Large parts of the city centre were destroyed by bombings during the second world war. In 1992 the Shanghai government relaxed the tax regime, which encouraged both foreign and domestic investment, resulting in subsequent annual economic growth of between 9 and 15%.

Housing Typologies

High rise dominates new construction, from centrally located luxury complexes to low-income towers on the peripheries. The concession districts remain low rise; a number of classic Lilongs, two- to four-storey terraced developments with internal streets, once prevalent from the 1840s to the 1990s, have received government protection, and mixed-use low-rise regeneration schemes are starting to appear in the city centre. Shanghai's new mid-density satellite towns demonstrate the Chinese penchant for European design, mimicking iconic elements of European cities in new urban street patterns.

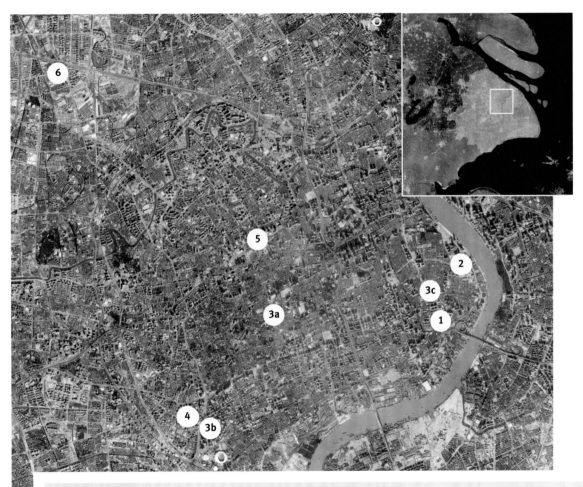

CASE STUDIES (*interview based)

PROJECT TYPE	ADDRESS	BUILD DATE
* 1 Shikumen House, classic Longtang dwelling	10 Shang Wen Road, Old Town, Huang Pu District	1935
* 2 New-build high rise	The Bund Side, Bai Du Road, Huang Pu District	2007
3 Courtyard and Garden Lilong housing	(a) Luwan District, (b) Xuhui District and (c) Old Town city centre	1930s and 1940s
4 (a) Traditional Apartment style Lilong houses	Xuhui District	1850s–1950s
(b) Modern Lilong houses	Portman House, Jianyeli, Xuhui District	1950s, remodelled 2011
5 Top of the City, High Rise	Wei hai Road, Jing An District	2005
6 Anting German town	Anting German Town, Jiading District	2005

1 Shikumen House, Classic Longtang Dwelling

Residents: Mr Rong and extended family
10 Shang Wen Road, Old Town, Huang Pu District

Lilong (or Longtang) housing is an urban community dwelling form: 'li' means community and 'long' means lanes. This terraced Shikumen (or stone gate) house was built in 1935 and 92-year-old Mr Rong has resided here since the end of the second world war in 1945.

Density and urban form

Characterised by semi-private lanes integrated into urban street blocks, Lilong communities achieve surprisingly high densities. Shops occupy the street frontages, while house entrances and shared amenities are organised off narrow courtyards running perpendicular to the central internal lane, separating the city's activities from private residential life. The shops, arches and stone gates mark the gradual transitions of privacy: from city (shops) to community (arches and lanes) to home (Shikumen).

Dwelling Plans

Above: Mr and Mrs Rong

Key:

A   Secondary entrance
B   Bedroom
C   Kitchen
D   Storage
E   Living
F   Traditional 'Shikumen entrance
G   Patio and garden
H   Side patio
I   Roof terrace

0m 1 2 3 4 5

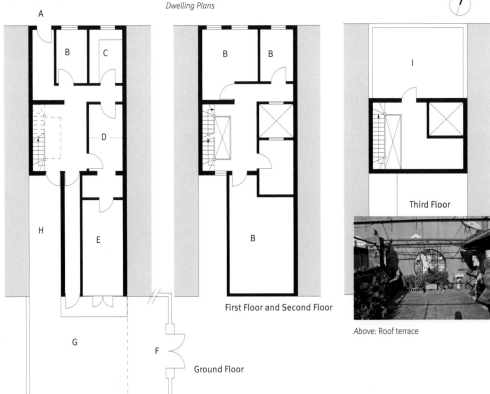

Ground Floor

First Floor and Second Floor

Third Floor

Above: Roof terrace

Flexibility and adaptability

In the course of its 77-year history, the house has been a family home, a refuge and a Japanese police station; the larger rooms accommodated these diverse functions without significant alteration. Mr Rong lives with 10 family members, yet the house could be divided into three apartments with relative ease. The roof terrace and external courtyard also provide opportunities to extend.

Appearance and threshold

The different facades of the Shikumen house present degrees of grandeur and privacy, with the main stone gate entrance usually facing south. Engravings identify the owner and express pride in the house. During the 1840s, a fusion of Chinese and European cultures influenced the architecture of Lilong houses: behind the oriental stone gate lies a British terraced house; elegantly proportioned openings and facade decoration are influenced by French art deco.

Space and light

The family living room opens directly onto a south-facing private courtyard garden. Tall timber doors can be fully opened, allowing light to flood into the central and most favoured space for the family. Generous floor-to-ceiling heights of 3.86 metres make the spaces feel expansive.

Construction and sustainability

Constructed in concrete and brick, the thermal mass keeps the house warm in the winter months and cool during the very hot Shanghai summers, while high ceilings and tall window openings to the front and back of the house allow natural cross ventilation.

Cost and value

A compact urban form, the Lilong terrace makes use of shared wall construction. The government owns and leases most of the existing unrenovated Lilongs to Chinese citizens at low rates. The renovated Lilongs, desirable family dwellings in the heart of the city, are sold as expatriate dwellings at significantly higher costs. Portman House Jian Ye Li (Case Study 4b) shows a successful adaptation of the classic Lilong ●

SCORES

DENSITY & URBAN FORM	17
FLEXIBILITY & ADAPTABILITY	17
APPEARANCE & THRESHOLD	18
SPACE & LIGHT	17
CONSTRUCTION & SUSTAINABILITY	7
TOTAL	76

Above left: Shikumen gate entrance

Above right: Interior view of the main room

CASE STUDY DATA

Density (HR/ha):	667
Plot ratio:	1.63:1
Cost to buy:	€4,800/m² (39,350 CNY/m²)*
Cost to rent/m²/m	€46/m²/m (380 CNY/m²/m)*
Buy cost as a multiple of average earnings:	x 206
Floor area:	245m²
Plot area:	150m²
Outdoor private amenity space:	22m² roof terrace and 52m² patio
Floor-to-ceiling height:	3.86m
Floor area per habitable room:	11m²
Age of building (and style):	1935, art deco terraced
Preferred room in the house:	Living space and patio

* Cost per square metre is based on similar renovated Shikumen houses sold in the Old Town in 2012

Internal street within the high-rise compound

2 **New-Build High Rise**

Resident: Guy Peters
The Bund Side, Bai Du Road, Huang Pu District

The Bund Side is archetypal Shanghai high-rise semi-luxury accommodation of between 10 and 31 storeys high, situated one metro stop from Shanghai's financial centre. Guy, 26, a German IT entrepreneur, has been renting a 16th-floor apartment for two years.

Density and urban form
Set in a 6-hectare landscaped compound, the towers occupy an area of 200,000 square metres. About 50% of the ground-floor area comprises greenery, making the plot ratio relatively low in relation to the block densities. The blocks are disconnected from the urban street network by the large gardens, reducing overshadowing from the adjoining blocks. All the semi-public areas are devoid of life, and commercial spaces at the base of the blocks remain unoccupied. Guy does not know anyone in his block .

Flexibility and adaptability
The spatial and functional arrangement is unalterable. The living room absorbs most of the space and bedrooms are cramped, so the apartment cannot accommodate a range of living patterns. Guy uses the apartment as a functional 'space to sleep'.

Dwelling Plan

Key:

A Bedroom
B Living
C Dining
D Kitchen
E Balcony

0m 1 2 3 4 5

SCORES	
DENSITY & URBAN FORM	4
FLEXIBILITY & ADAPTABILITY	5
APPEARANCE & THRESHOLD	7
SPACE & LIGHT	19
CONSTRUCTION & SUSTAINABILITY	1
TOTAL	36

Appearance and threshold
The design is 1990s mainstream modern, with crisp lines. Landscaping is used to soften the elevation at ground level and the compound format provides a feeling of security.

Space and light
The two-bedroom apartment, at 110m², is typical for Shanghai. It has a balcony providing panoramic views. The ceiling height is 2.68 metres; single aspect provides natural light to each habitable space. The apartment was clearly regarded as a temporary residence, like a hotel suite, with no personal items on display.

Construction and sustainability
The building is made of insulated brick set in a concrete frame with repetitive windows and balconies, which lowers construction costs. No renewable energy sources are used, but monthly utility costs for each apartment are low.

Cost and value
With an average 143% residential-property price growth from December 2005 to June 2011, speculative high-rise developments targeted at high earners are fuelling inflation and are now showing high vacancy rates – this despite a shortage of affordable inner-urban housing. In 2008, Guy's 110m² apartment cost 2m CNY (€250,000); it would currently cost 6.6m CNY (€787,294) – this is 141 times the average annual salary. A majority of Shanghai's existing properties continue to be owned and leased to residents by the local government and are relatively stable in price compared to the speculative market ●

CASE STUDY DATA

Density (HR/ha):	930
Plot ratio:	3.3:1
Cost to buy:	€7,320/m² (60,000 CNY/m²)
Cost to rent/m²/m	€9/m²/m (76 CNY/m²/m)
Buy cost as a multiple of average earnings:	x 141
Floor area:	110m²
Plot area:	60,000m²
Outdoor private amenity space:	5m² balcony and 6 hectares gardens
Floor-to-ceiling height:	2.68m
Floor area per habitable room:	27m²
Age of building (and style):	2007, modern high rise
Preferred room in the house:	Living room and balcony

Above left top: A vacant shop at ground floor level

Above left: Guy in his apartment

Above right: The spectacular view from Guy's apartment

Left: View of the courtyard housing entrance

Above: A launderette in an internal lane of Jing'An Villa

3 Courtyard and Garden Lilong Housing

Luwan District, Xuhui District, and Old Town city centre 1930s and 1940s

Built for wealthy international and Chinese families, these houses are large and well proportioned and achieve high densities; the terraced dwellings and small lanes make efficient use of land. Many properties were subdivided during the Cultural Revolution for social housing, and now accommodate up to 12 families per house. Overcrowding compromises the positive characteristics of such dense housing forms. The ground-floor areas of some properties now incorporate shops, launderettes and cafes.

SCORES	
DENSITY & URBAN FORM	20
FLEXIBILITY & ADAPTABILITY	11
APPEARANCE & THRESHOLD	16
SPACE & LIGHT	11
CONSTRUCTION & SUSTAINABILITY	3
TOTAL	61

4 (a) Traditional Apartment-style Lilong houses

Xuhui District 1850s–1950s

Built to house the influx of Chinese and foreign workers, these economically constructed dwellings are adaptations of the British town house to suit the Chinese community lifestyle. Two- to four-storey terraces clustered around internal alleyways create semi-private space. This configuration achieves high densities in low-rise blocks. Lilongs housed more than 80% of the population by 1945, but since the 1990s many have been demolished to make way for high-rise developments.

Right: Entrance to low-income Lilong

Far right: Modernised lane houses

SCORES	
DENSITY & URBAN FORM	20
FLEXIBILITY & ADAPTABILITY	10
APPEARANCE & THRESHOLD	19
SPACE & LIGHT	11
CONSTRUCTION & SUSTAINABILITY	3
TOTAL	63

(b) Modern Lilong houses

Portman House, Jianyeli, Xuhui District 1950s, remodelled 2011

More recently, this simple housing form is regaining popularity. Portman House Jianyeli is a Lilong renovation with basements added to intensify its urban density. Originally a modest residential development, it now boasts luxury serviced apartments, residential units and over 3,716 square metres of retail space.

5 Top of the City, High Rise
Wei hai Road, Jing An District 2005

With its centrally located luxury tower blocks, the so-called 'Top of City' is composed of apartments ranging from 70m² (7,900 CNY/€950 pcm) to 166m² (25,000 CNY/€3,000 pcm). The blocks are surrounded by gardens with an artificial lake, yielding a plot ratio of 2.5:1 (a figure similar to the low-rise Lilong communities) in accordance with new government measures to control overdevelopment.

SCORES	
DENSITY & URBAN FORM	4
FLEXIBILITY & ADAPTABILITY	8
APPEARANCE & THRESHOLD	4
SPACE & LIGHT	16
CONSTRUCTION & SUSTAINABILITY	0
TOTAL	32

Left: Top of City

6 Anting German Town
Anting German Town, Jiading District 2005

Situated in the heart of China's automotive-industry district, this German-themed mixed-use development is part of Shanghai's 'One City, Nine Towns Plan' to relieve housing pressures in the centre. Designed by architect Albert Speer to accommodate 50,000 inhabitants, the town remains two-thirds vacant seven years after it was constructed.

SCORES	
DENSITY & URBAN FORM	13
FLEXIBILITY & ADAPTABILITY	8
APPEARANCE & THRESHOLD	10
SPACE & LIGHT	16
CONSTRUCTION & SUSTAINABILITY	8
TOTAL	55

German Town: centre

Security guards protect the uninhabited and decaying new-build houses

PART 3: PROTOTYPE

Introduction to Part 3, and Findings

Our quest to find durable and appealing housing types that could be scaled to create successful urban communities, based on our research tour from Mexico City to Tokyo, yielded diverse conclusions, summarised in earlier chapters. From the many examples we looked at, we selected 62 homes as case studies, with at least six in each of the nine cities. In each city there was one typology (and in some cases more than one) that could be said to qualify as an archetype in the sense described in the Introduction: a type of home that is a recognised and much-loved classic, and one that we would expect to perform very well against the 25 criteria in the evaluation.

These types were as follows (chapter number/case study):

> **Copenhagen:** Kartoffelraekkerne (8/1)
>
> **Melbourne:** Victorian terrace houses (9/1)
>
> **Tokyo:** Traditional houses (10/5)
>
> **London:** Georgian terraces (11/2)
>
> **New York:** Brownstones (12/1)
>
> **Paris:** Post-Haussmann flats (13/1)
>
> **Berlin:** Altbauwohnungen (14/1)
>
> **Mexico City:** Vecindades (15/1)
>
> **Shanghai:** Lilong houses (16/1)

The evaluations produced very interesting results. When all criteria were used, including performance against construction and sustainability questions, the highest scoring type was a new scheme of terraced houses built by the Danish government outside Copenhagen (8/6). Although slightly below ideal density, this scored highly in all areas. The lowest-scoring schemes were the high-rise flats in Tokyo (10/4), which although dense were poor in almost every other regard, and the infamous Colonias Populares in Mexico City, which although dire were at least constructed as communities and were being improved. A list of the top nine performers with scores follows (marks out of 100):

Danish affordable housing, Copenhagen (8/5):	84*
Baugruppe, Esmarchstrasse, Berlin (14/2):	83*
Kartoffelraekkerne Copenhagen (8/1):	81
Modscape prefabricated houses, Melbourne (9/5):	79*
Lilong (Shikumen) house, Shanghai (16/1):	76
Social housing, Paris (13/3):	65*
Vecindad Ideal, Mexico City (15/1):	76
Victorian terraced housing, Melbourne (9/1):	76
Georgian terraced house, London (11/2):	75

(* indicates new-build scheme)

The older buildings generally scored less well against criteria in the areas of construction method and sustainability than did the newer schemes. If these criteria are stripped away, leaving a comparison of all the buildings merely as habitation (which presumably could be constructed to modern standards), then the scores were as follows (marks out of 80):

Kartoffelraekkerne Copenhagen (8/1):	74
Vecindad Ideal, Mexico City (15/1):	73
Classic brownstone, New York (12/1):	72
Georgian terraced house, London (11/2):	71
Victorian terraced housing, Melbourne (9/1):	71
Danish affordable housing, Copenhagen (8/5):	67*
Lilong (Shikumen) house, Shanghai (16/1):	69
Terraced housing, Butte aux Cailles, Paris (13/6):	69
Mews House, London (11/8):	68

(* indicates new-build scheme)

Other notable newer housing projects that were included as case studies for comparison scored in the mid range as follows (marks out of 100):

Moriyama House and United Cubes, Tokyo (10/6):	71*
New urban housing, Donnybrook Quarter, London (11/6):	60*
New urban housing, Evelyn Road, London (11/7):	59*
Prefabricated housing, Murray Grove, London (11/5):	53*
Mountain Dwellings, Copenhagen (8/2):	49*
Tiergarten and Lützowufer, Berlin (14/6):	50*
Top of City, Shanghai (16/5):	32*
High-rise apartments, New York (12/4):	31*
Eureka Tower, Melbourne (9/4):	27*

(* indicates new-build scheme)

Full sets of the evaluation spreadsheets for all the case studies are available using the associated QR icon at the start of the City chapters.

The questions used for the evaluations were constructed as far as possible so that answers would be unequivocal and subjectivity minimised (see Introduction to Part 2). However, the scorings have not been scientifically weighted, and they should be regarded as indicative rather than precise. They do nevertheless give an interesting general picture: housing based on refined archetypal building forms scores highest, followed by innovative modern schemes – and both perform better than new and postwar high-rise blocks.

Part 3 describes how we applied the findings of our research to the problem of designing and creating an idealised urban house type, a new prototype.

Vecindad Ideal, Mexico City: one of the best-scoring archetypes

CHAPTER 17: MAKING A HOUSE IN THE CITY

We asked ourselves the question: 'What would a modern house, built in London where we live, which satisfies all of our criteria and which displays the best of the most successful attributes we uncovered from our case studies, actually look like?' Rather than simply designing a prototype on paper, we decided to find a site and build our own model house. We wanted a site in the city proper, with all the attendant real-world challenges: noise and pollution, proximity with neighbours, overlooking and rights-of-light issues, ground contamination, town planning constraints and the requirements of local construction legislation. It was also clearly a requirement that this house could be sold and occupied in a conventional property market (Fig. 17.01).

The story of making a house in the city

Suitable sites for new stand-alone houses in London proved to be rare indeed, but through friends we found a plot in Hammersmith (an inner London borough), at the end of a terrace near a high street, large enough for a single house. The plot was vacant and small (about 9 metres by 9 metres), just enough space to park three cars – and it was bounded on three sides. On the face of it, this was a challenging configuration, but we had already developed the bones of a prototype capable of relatively high densities that could be inserted into difficult terraced situations such as this: much shallower than the typical London plot, which is normally about 20 metres deep.

The prototype on paper

The basis of the prototype is illustrated here (Fig. 17.02).

We take a rectangle of about 4.5 metres square internally, double it in plan and then give the whole plan a height of about 3 metres. The volume thereby created must be clear span, so that it can be used freely as bedroom or living or office space, or can incorporate kitchens or bathrooms if appropriate vertical services are supplied. One cube in the plan has windows facing the street. The other is given windows on the flank wall facing a courtyard. In this way, a building of 9 metres depth and bounded at the rear can be created. A second block is positioned to the side, and this forms the entrance and encloses a detached staircase. It also forms an enclosing wall to the courtyard.

This simple plan form can be stacked up to three storeys above ground without the need for a lift, and can also be developed with

Fig. 17.01: The site as found

Fig. 17.02: Prototype development

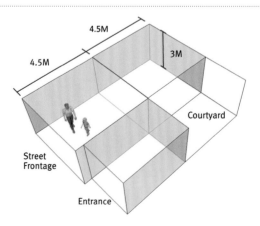

basement space. When on multiple levels the total floor area can be used as one dwelling, or it can easily be subdivided into separate compartments floor by floor, because the staircase is separated from the open-plan floor space.

We configured the top level with the back half of the house open as a roof terrace and the front half enclosed as habitable space set behind a pitched roof.

Learning from the case studies

Below, we use the chapter headings from Part 1 to explain how the prototype design follows the lessons learned from the case studies and from the criteria that we generated

Density and Urban form

The basic prototype design – two full storeys above ground – with a second-floor room next to the roof terrace, and with a full basement, yields a total internal floor area of about 150 square metres, a density of about 500 HR/ha and a plot ratio of about 1.5:1, when developed on the Hammersmith plot. The prototype plan form can be organised in terraces to form streets, mews courts and squares, and crucially can be constructed with houses arranged both side-by-side and back-to-back, thus preserving what is a relatively high density even when scaled up to form a city quarter including access roads, parking and open space (Fig.17.03).

At the end of the chapter we have illustrated how the prototype can be expressed in a number of different ways, by the addition of storeys and by using a variety of configurations of access lanes and streets. These examples include approximations of a number of the archetypal homes that were found.

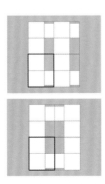

Fig.17.03: City streets and squares

Flexibility and Adaptability

The size of a typical 'cell', its plan and section, and the absence of loadbearing partitions allows the widest possible range of uses. With the house in Hammersmith we created three locations for vertical services, so that kitchens and/or bathrooms could be located in any one of three places on any floor.

Windows to the principal spaces are identical and spaced regularly, so that the floor space is undifferentiated, and subdivisible. These characteristics directly address the requirements we identified for flexibility and adaptability (see Chapter 3) (Fig. 17.04).

And as noted above, the arrangement of the staircase, independent of the clear-span space, makes it possible to subdivide the house by floor (so it is permeable, using the term described in Chapter 3). We managed to sell the house in Hammersmith off-plan, so were able to work with the eventual owners during the latter design stages. They opted to use the entire basement as one large family room – kitchen, dining and living space together – with direct access to the courtyard. Then a master-bedroom suite was created on the ground floor, with bedrooms for children and guests on the first floor, and a family study area at second-floor level next to the roof terrace. But the owners expect to relocate to Canada or the US within five years, so there was a requirement that the house should be capable of reconfiguration as two maisonettes, one for them to retain as a pied-à-terre. The concept on which the prototype was based is in fact capable of a wide variety of interpretations, so we were able to accommodate their vision (Fig. 17.05). Options for commercial office and/or retail space at ground level, with residential space above are also possible with the prototype concept (Fig.17.06).

First Floor

Second Floor

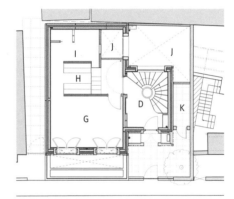

Ground Floor

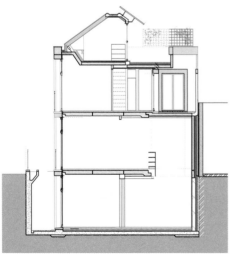

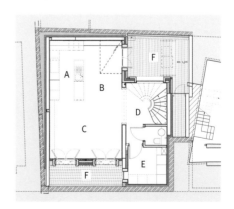

Basement Level

Fig. 17.04: Biscay Road house, drawings

Key:

A   Kitchen
B   Dining
C   Living
D   Stairwell/entrance to terrace
E   Utility
F   Terrace
G   Bedroom
H   Dressing
I   Bathroom
J   Lightwell
K   Bike storage
L   Study/Bedroom

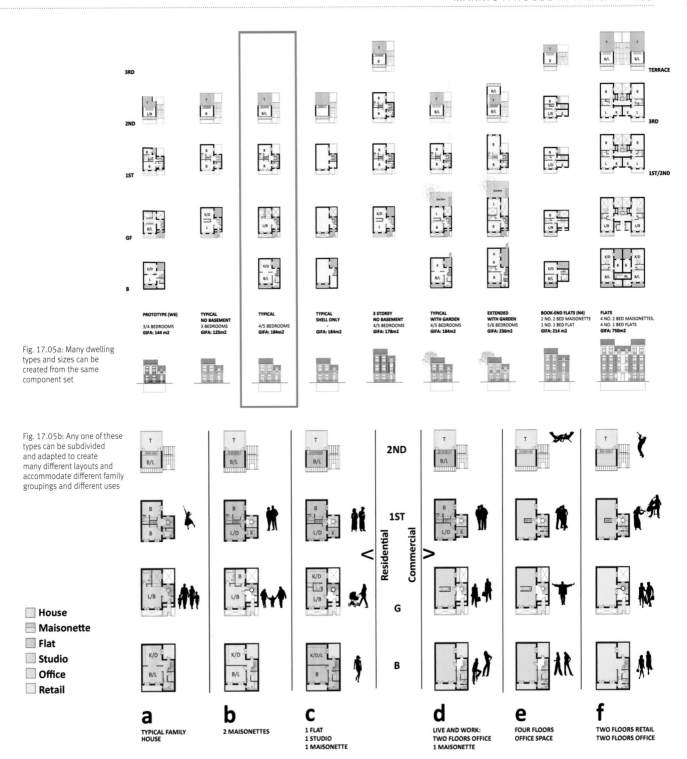

Fig. 17.05a: Many dwelling types and sizes can be created from the same component set

	PROTOTYPE (W6)	TYPICAL NO BASEMENT	TYPICAL	TYPICAL SHELL ONLY	3 STOREY NO BASEMENT	TYPICAL WITH GARDEN	EXTENDED WITH GARDEN	BOOK-END FLATS (N4)	FLATS
	3/4 bedrooms	3 BEDROOMS	4/5 BEDROOMS	-	4/5 BEDROOMS	4/5 BEDROOMS	5/6 BEDROOMS	2 NO. 2 BED MAISONETTE 1 NO. 1 BED FLAT	4 NO. 2 BED MAISONETTES, 4 NO. 1 BED FLATS
	GIFA: 144 m2	GIFA: 125m2	GIFA: 184m2	GIFA: 184m2	GIFA: 178m2	GIFA: 184m2	GIFA: 236m2	GIFA: 214 m2	GIFA: 750m2

Fig. 17.05b: Any one of these types can be subdivided and adapted to create many different layouts and accommodate different family groupings and different uses

- House
- Maisonette
- Flat
- Studio
- Office
- Retail

a TYPICAL FAMILY HOUSE

b 2 MAISONETTES

c 1 FLAT 1 STUDIO 1 MAISONETTE

d LIVE AND WORK: TWO FLOORS OFFICE 1 MAISONETTE

e FOUR FLOORS OFFICE SPACE

f TWO FLOORS RETAIL TWO FLOORS OFFICE

Fig. 17.07: Both the Georgian proportioning system and the Golden Rectangle are used to regulate the facade (see Chapter 4, Appearance & Threshold)

Appearance and Threshold

The prototype is an expression of our conclusion that high-density low-rise development is the most durable and successful model for urban residential development. Terraces made from the prototype house create a pleasant and familiar street scene, and arrangements of three- and four-storey versions of the model, in squares and mews courts of an attractive scale, are also easily achieved.

In considering the design of the elevations, we were concerned to provide generous openings but conscious of the need to conserve energy. The placement of windows was governed by two systems of proportion: the geometry of the typical Georgian facade (as described by Cruickshank, Chapter 4), and the regulating lines of the Golden Rectangle (Fig. 17.07).

The house is separated from the street by a light well serving one side of the basement room, a device typical of older buildings in London that allows houses to be placed close to the pavement but preserves a sense of detachment. The entrance is recessed under cover, and set in a private gated forecourt. We felt that this arrangement created a comfortable sequence in the transition from public to private worlds. As the house in Hammersmith is very near a major London artery, this formality seemed to be necessary. If the house had been in a lane off a side street then the approach could have been much more relaxed, and the forecourt area could have formed a semi-public extension to the living space – a feature so successful in the terraced housing of Copenhagen.

Space and Light

The relationships between room size, height, depth and window size for the model house in Hammersmith generally follow our conclusions (Chapter 5). However, we were obliged to reduce the height of the second floor and part of the first-floor space in order to satisfy planning requirements associated with the adjoining roof ridge line; and we had to provide a private balcony to the guest bedroom at the back of the property to avoid compromising privacy and established rights of light.

Nevertheless, the prototype window design, based on the classic Parisian pattern of long inward-opening casements with openable fanlights set behind narrow shutters, is uniformly employed across the street elevation, and this format conveys the intentions of the prototype design both internally and externally. From inside there are good views of the sky and of the street, whether a person is standing or sitting. The reveals are deep, discreetly housing the shutters when they are folded away. The impression inside is one of spaciousness, light and solidity. Windows and shutters can be adjusted to filter sunlight and view and air, so they adapt to suit temperament and weather and time of day (Fig. 17.08).

Fig. 17.08: The principal family room, and the master bedroom

Outdoor space for a family home is essential, but providing it on a site so small is a challenge. In the end, we were able to create more than 36 square metres of private amenity space, aggregating the courtyard and roof-terrace areas. This space represents almost half the plan area of the original plot, illustrating the good sense of creating private roof terraces as a high-density alternative to back gardens (Fig. 17.09).

Construction and Sustainability

For our model house, we set ourselves the target of reaching Level 4 defined by the UK Code for Sustainable Homes as an acceptable standard relating to, among other things, carbon emissions, energy consumption and responsible sourcing of materials. This standard is well above the current UK Building Regulations requirement, but it is expected to be mandatory in the near future. We achieved this level by ensuring that the building enclosure was very well insulated and airtight, by incorporating a mechanical ventilation system with heat exchange/recovery capability, and by introducing a photovoltaic array at roof level, capable of generating about 15% of the total electricity requirement for the house.

In terms of the construction process, we were interested to research the characteristics of off-site manufacture and its associated benefits in terms of quality of product, speed of assembly on site and improvements in the working conditions of those physically involved in construction. We were also keen to establish what cost reductions could be achieved by creating a system of components that could be assembled in a variety of standard patterns reflecting the aspirations of our prototype model in terms of proportions, solidity and architectural expression. Low maintenance of the finished building was also a priority, suggested particularly by social landlords.

For the Hammersmith building, the primary structure and building skin were combined in a system known as sandwich

Fig. 17.09: The courtyard and the roof terrace: a combined area of 36 square metres of private outside amenity space on a tiny plot

construction, in which the enclosing walls are made up of panels consisting of two skins of cast stone (architectural concrete) with a thick layer of rigid insulation between them. The intermediate floors, flat roof and staircases were also precast in factories, and the entire system was assembled and bolted together with steel cleats at the rate of about eight panels per day. For a typical house, the assembly process would therefore take roughly two weeks to complete, but we extended the assembly period to about six weeks given the experimental nature of the project. Windows were preassembled complete with glazing and ironmongery, and fitted into precast

window surrounds in the factory (Fig. 17.10).

The precast panels, floor and staircases were formed using natural aggregates and, where external, the choice of sand, aggregate and cement has created the required variations in panel colour (which will require no maintenance). Inner structural skins and other internal components, including floors and staircases, were made from so-called secondary (or recycled) aggregates, and in total about 76% of the volume of all the primary structural and cladding components was made up of what is effectively industrial waste.

Fig. 17.10: Under construction

Credits for design
Architecture and interior design - Rational House Limited
Sustainability and mechanical design - Arup
Structural design - Kevin Elliott

Credits for construction
Primary structure and cladding - Sterling Services Limited (UK)
Staircases - Cornish Concrete Limited (UK)
Windows - NorDan (Norway)
Shutters - AST (Austria)
Mechanical services - Elmec Limited (UK)
Fit out and electrical services - C&H Hawkings Limited (UK)
Specialist joinery - Harry James Limited (UK)

Moving In
As explained earlier, the owners, Nathan and Jennifer, worked with us throughout the fit-out period, and together with them we devised a layout of rooms and a fit-out specification that suited their family lifestyle and budget. Many options were discussed before the final details were agreed.

The construction work was completed in December 2011, enabling them to move into the house just before Christmas, so that as we go to press on this book they have been living in and enjoying the house for over 9 months. Nathan in particular has been a great supporter of the Rational House concept, and has taken interest in every detail of the project and in our novel approach. We continue to have regular conversations with the family, and now that we are clear of the defects period, we are bringing into effect a monitoring system that will keep an eye on the performance of the house, particularly on the consumption of gas and electricity, and on the effectiveness of the photovoltaic panels.

So far Nathan and Jennifer say they are very happy, and we are delighted to have found such an enthusiastic and appropriate client for our first pilot project.

Above: Nathan, Jennifer, Jacqueline and Spencer

Rational house as archetype

The illustrations below show how the concept model can be arranged to achieve the best characteristics of each of the housing types listed. A new company, City House Projects, has been established to enable the building of Rational House communities. (www.rationalhouse.com)

Rational House as Shanghai Lilong Houses

Density: 546 HR/ha (three-storey houses) or 703 HR/ha (four-storey houses)

Plot Ratio: 1.6: 1 (three-storey houses) or 2.1: 1 (four-storey houses)

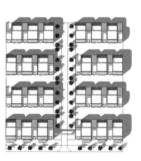

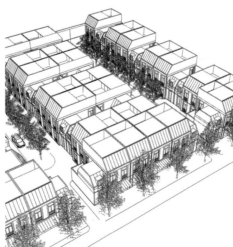

Rational House as Mexico City Vencidades
(or London Mews Houses)

Density: 416 HR/ha (two-storey houses) or 583 HR/ha (with basements)

Plot Ratio: 1.2:1 (two-storey houses) or 1.7:1 (with basements)

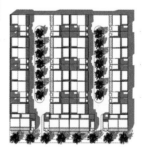

Fig. 17.11: Archetype drawings

Rational House as Copenhagen Potato Row Houses
(or small London Georgian houses)

Density: 333 HR/ha (two-storey houses)
or 466 (with basements)

Plot Ratio: 1.0:1 (two-storey houses)
or 1.5:1 (with basements)

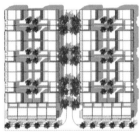
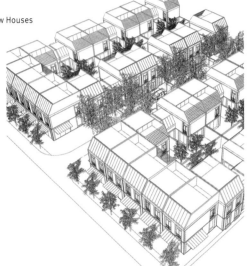

Rational House as Berlin Altbau
(or Paris Haussmann flats)

Density: 629 HR/ha (four-storey flats)
or 815 HR/ha (five-storey flats)

Plot Ratio: 1.8:1 (four-storey flats)
or 2.2:1 (five-storey flats)

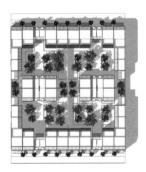
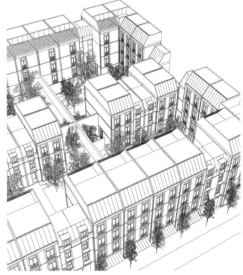

In conclusion

In the context of acute housing need, there is a place for a housing product that one could call the city house. This concept could flourish in the urban zone that encircles larger cities (neither suburban nor central). The city house would be high density but low rise, very flexible and adaptable, generous, well-proportioned, sustainable, constructed economically using modern methods, and built with 'soft edges' and configured in streets and squares. Housing concepts from the past, such as the European concessions in Shanghai, the vecindades in Mexico and the terraced 'potato racks' of Copenhagen, have shown that it is possible to create durable housing types that address many of these requirements and that are also transportable into different urban settings and cultural environments.

Our own proposal for a city house is not a mechanical translation of these findings; it is only one of the possible approaches. But it is one that has tried to embrace all the important design influences we identified rather than a limited number of them; it has done so in a real city, and it has been conceived so that the solution can be scaled, repeated and applied in widely different circumstances.

Fig. 17.06: Biscay Road: in context

Contributors

(in order of appearance in the book)

Tim Battle, editor

Tim is a Founder Director of Rational House Limited, and chairman of City
House Projects Limited, the implementation vehicle for Rational House concepts.
He was previously a director of the engineering consultancy company Rybka Battle,
pathfinders in energy-conscious and sustainable design.

David Lunts, Foreword

David is the Executive Director for Housing and Land at the GLA
where he leads the mayor's new housing, land and development functions.
He was previously the Executive Director for London at the Homes and Communities Agency.
He had a leading role in housing and regeneration in Manchester during the 1980s and a
three-year spell as director of Urban Policy at the Office of the Deputy Prime Minister.

Stuart Hallett, Chapter 6 on sustainability

Stuart is a senior engineer with Arup, with particular expertise and interest in matters of
sustainability, energy and CO_2 appraisal. He was the project engineer for the prototype
Rational House (Chapter 17).

Ben de Waal, Chapter 7 on cost

Ben is Head of Residential at Davis Langdon, an AECOM Company. He is also a key partner
in the Rational House team, and a non-executive director of City House Projects Limited.
Ben's primary focus has been on the presentation of a robust commercial offer and the
development of a scalable supply chain for the Rational House product.

Yolande Barnes, Chapter 7 on value

Yolande is Head of Residential Research at Savills. Her work involves providing
thought leadership and running a department to provide sophisticated, market-oriented
advice on all aspects of residential real estate, and leadership on strategic and policy issues.
Yolande is also a director of Design for Homes and a founding member of the
Society of Property Researchers.

Acknowledgements

The Authors would like to thank:

Our close colleagues and families:

Tim Battle for his energy and unwavering commitment to the project.

Joe Cefai of Sterling Services for his ingenuity and generosity of spirit.

Amy Charles and **Mary Battle** for their invaluable help and guidance.

Jon Charles for his beautiful photography and for his friendship.

Our partners, **Louise Coubrough** and **Clement Cortale,** for their unfailing support and patience.

The Contributors, and **Michael Carley**, whose ideas have expanded the breadth of our understanding.

Friends and collaborators who helped us to find our way in nine world cities:

Nanna Kallenbach (Copenhagen); Jessica Olanda and Tom Sullivan (Melbourne); Hiromi Watanabe, Robert Schmidt III, Toru Eguchi, and Professor Shuichi Matsumura (Tokyo); Cliff Tapp (New York); Sophie Wiggie (Paris); Peter Dassel, Nico Degenkolb, Julia Leihener, and Malte Reimer (Berlin); Fernando Tapia, James Leatham, Juan Pablo Maza and Juan Reyes (Mexico City); JG Chen, Patrick JW Allen, Squirrel Qi, Peter Sailer, James Macdonald, Giel Groothuis and Alvaro Leonardo (Shanghai).

The wonderful people who allowed us to come into their homes, and who shared their ideas with us:

Svend Larsen and Jane & Thomas Ziegler (Copenhagen); Tom & Marie Keel and Mary Olanda (Melbourne); Toshihiro & Yumiko Okamoto and Kenji Kimoto (Tokyo); Irina Nazarenko and Justin & Sam Sayer (London); Julia de Roulet, O Zhang & Peter Garfield, Jean-Luc Fievet and Ed Bennett (New York); Emilie & Christophe Gronen and Deirdre & Michael Guzy (Paris); Professor Christof Helberger, Jutta Kraemer and Carsten & Ulrike Probst (Berlin); Mariana & Abraham Gonzales, Sofia & Jorge Villarreal, Lorenzo Alvarez & Carolina Pichet and Megali & Daniel Pence (Mexico City); Mr & Mrs Rong and Guy Knipping (Shanghai).

Nathan Brown and Jennifer Weitzel, the owners of the first prototype Rational House in west London. They have been such enthusiastic partners throughout the project, and they continue to be great supporters of the initiative.

Aubrey Newman for helping us to find a suitable site for the prototype, and for his encouragement along the way.

And finally, may we express our thanks to the directors, staff and consultants at RIBA Publishing, in particular Matthew Thompson for his vision and tenacity; to Lucy Harbor, Kate Mackillop and Sharon Hodgson for their wisdom and thoroughness; and to Ashley Western for his brilliant page settings.

Picture Credits

DIVIDER

68/69   © Sheila Qureshi Cortale

COLLAGE

72/73   All © Jonathan Charles

CHAPTER 8

74	© Jonathan Charles
75	© TerraServer.com
76	© TerraServer.com
76	© Plans: Rational House
77	© Jonathan Charles
78	© TerraServer.com
78	© Plan: Rational House
78	© Jonathan Charles
79	© Jonathan Charles
80	© Jonathan Charles
81	© Jonathan Charles

CHAPTER 9

82	© Jonathan Charles
83	© TerraServer.com
84	© TerraServer.com
84	© Plans: Rational House
84	© Jonathan Charles
85	© Jonathan Charles
86	© TerraServer.com
86	© Plan: Rational House
86	© Jonathan Charles
87	© Jonathan Charles
88	© Jonathan Charles
89	© Jonathan Charles

CHAPTER 10

90	© Jonathan Charles
91	© TerraServer.com
92	© TerraServer.com
92	© Plan: Rational House
92	© Jonathan Charles
93	© Jonathan Charles
94	© TerraServer.com
94	© Plans: Rational House
94	© Jonathan Charles
95	© Jonathan Charles
96	© Jonathan Charles
97	© Jonathan Charles

CHAPTER 11

98	© Jonathan Charles
99	© TerraServer.com
100	© TerraServer.com
100	© Plans: Rational House
100	© Jonathan Charles
101	© Jonathan Charles
102	© TerraServer.com
102	© Plans: Rational House
102	© Jonathan Charles
103	© Jonathan Charles
104	© Jonathan Charles
105	© Jonathan Charles
106	© Visual: Peter Barber Architects
106	© Photo: Jonathan Charles
107	© Jonathan Charles

CHAPTER 12

108	© Jonathan Charles
109	© TerraServer.com
110	© TerraServer.com
110	© Plans: Rational House
110	© Jonathan Charles
111	© Jonathan Charles
112	© TerraServer.com
112	© Jonathan Charles
113	© Plans: Rational House
113	© Photos: Jonathan Charles
114	© Jonathan Charles
115	© Jonathan Charles
116	© Jonathan Charles
117	© Jonathan Charles

CHAPTER 13

118	© Jonathan Charles
119	© TerraServer.com
120	© TerraServer.com
120	© Plan: Rational House
120	© Jonathan Charles
121	© Jonathan Charles
122	© TerraServer.com
122	© Jonathan Charles
123	© Plan: Rational House
123	© Jonathan Charles
124	© Jonathan Charles
125	© Jonathan Charles

CHAPTER 14

126	© Jonathan Charles
127	© TerraServer.com
128	© TerraServer.com
128	© Jonathan Charles
129	© Plan: Rational House
129	© Jonathan Charles
130	© Jonathan Charles
131	© Jonathan Charles
132	© TerraServer.com

132	© Plan: Rational House
132	© Jonathan Charles
133	© Jonathan Charles
134	© Jonathan Charles
135	© Jonathan Charles

CHAPTER 15

136	© Jonathan Charles
137	© TerraServer.com
138	© TerraServer.com
138	© Plans: Rational House
138	© Jonathan Charles
139	© Jonathan Charles
140	© TerraServer.com
140	© Jonathan Charles
141	© Rational House
142	© Jonathan Charles
143	© Jonathan Charles

CHAPTER 16

144	© Jonathan Charles
145	© TerraServer.com
146	© TerraServer.com
146	© Plans: Rational House
146	© Jonathan Charles
147	© Jonathan Charles
148	© TerraServer.com
148	© Plan: Rational House
148	© Jonathan Charles
149	© Jonathan Charles
150	© Jonathan Charles
151	© Jonathan Charles

DIVIDER

152/153 © Jonathan Charles

155 · © Jonathan Charles

CHAPTER 17

156	Fig 17.01	© Jonathan Charles
156	Fig 17.02	© Rational House
157	Fig 17.03	© Rational House
158	Fig 17.04	© Rational House
159	Fig 17.05a & b	© Rational House
160	Fig 17.07	© Jonathan Charles and Rational House
161	Fig 17.08	© Jonathan Charles
162/63	Fig 17.09	© Jonathan Charles
164	Fig 17.10	© Jonathan Charles
165		© Jonathan Charles
166/67		© Rational House
169	Fig 17.06	© Jonathan Charles

Index

...so, how do we want to live?